Breathing Again
   ... thoughts on life after loss

Also by Cathy Marley

Peeking Over the Edge ... views from life's middle, 2006

Love in Bloom
  with Women Writers of the Desert, 2005

Breathing Again
... thoughts on life after loss

Cathy Marley

Press

Copyright © 2018 by Cathy Marley

All rights reserved. No part of this book shall be reproduced or transmitted in any form or by any means, electronic, mechanical, magnetic, photographic including photocopying, recording or by any information storage and retrieval system, without prior written permission of the publisher or author. No patent liability is assumed with respect to the use of the information contained herein. Although every precaution has been taken in the preparation of this book, the publisher and author assume no responsibility for errors or omissions. Neither is any liability assumed for damages resulting from the use of the information contained herein.

Reviewers may quote passages for use in periodicals, newspapers, or broadcasts provided credit is given to Breathing Again by Cathy Marley. Contact: Cathy Marley at CJM@CathyMarley.com.

This is a work of non-fiction and names have been used with permission.

ISBN 978-0-9990518-0-1

Cover photography by Cathy Marley
Content photography © Cathy Marley except where noted
Author photo: Leanna McDonald, www.photosbyleanna.com
6 Principles of From Grief to Peace © From Grief to Peace, LLC

Published by:

CJM Press,
Phoenix, AZ
www.CathyMarley.com
Email CJM@CathyMarley.com

Printed in the United States of America

Printed on Recycled Paper

Published January 2018

For Norm, my soul mate, my love, my joy,
the center of my world.

and

For Dale and Anita,
precious son and beloved soul sister.
We will meet again.

Acknowledgments

Writing is of necessity a solitary endeavor. But, as any author will tell you, no book is ever created in a vacuum. The path from three women starting a book club to my publishing *Breathing Again* was a long one—filled with education, inspiration, compassion, and yes, sometimes even tears. Grief is not an easy topic to write about, and I am convinced *Breathing Again* would never have been written without the inspiration, support, and input from some of the strongest, most resilient people I know.

As always, I thank my wonderful husband Norm, whose faith in me has never wavered. With every word I wrote here, I became ever more grateful to have had you in my life for over forty years. Every moment I spent learning from others what it means to truly grieve left me praying I would be granted many more years with you and never have to know the pain of living without you or those three incredible human beings, David, Dale, and Dennie, who I have been privileged to call "my" children.

Sadly, before I could finish this book, I learned firsthand more than I ever wanted to know about consuming grief and its many side effects when our precious son, Dale, succumbed to cancer a scant five months after diagnosis. It was a loss I neither expected nor wanted to know. Fortunately, most of *Breathing Again* was written before he died. In writing it, I had gained precious insights on grief from others and had incorporated them here. What I had learned helped me through that soul-numbing time as I had come to understand that what I was experiencing was normal and to be expected. Once I was able to return to writing, I felt our son's spiritual presence guiding me to its completion. Thank you, Dale.

So much of what I have learned about grief, I learned from two amazing and inspiring women, my dear friends and soul sisters, Joy Collins and Betts McCalla. You shared your pain, your sorrow, and your experiences with me, and I hear your voices echo in the pages here. Many of the stories you voiced over chai tea lattes and coffee at the Barnes and Noble café have found their way into this book. In a sense, what I have written mirrors your path from grief to peace. I send my deepest thanks to you both for all of that and for guiding me through designing, editing, formatting, and publishing *Breathing Again*.

Finally, to the sisters of my heart, Anita and Elaine, one on this side of the veil, the other waiting to welcome us to the other side when our time comes, I can only say that without your years of love and encouragement, I would never have had the courage to start writing in the first place. We've come a long way, haven't we? And the best is yet to come when we are all together again!

Thank you, one and all.

Cathy Marley

Table of Contents

Foreword *1*
Introduction *3*
6 Principles of From Grief to Peace *7*
Breathing Again *9*
Chapter 1 Is This Really Happening? *15*
   What Works for You 17
   The Widowed Box 21
   Would You Want to Know? 25
   Get Over It? The Constant Weight of Grief 27
   Oh, I Get by with a Little Help 33

Chapter 2 How You Feel *37*
   Walls – Protection or Prison? 39
   I'm Fine 43
   The Ka-thunk 47
   Do I Still Matter? 51
   Touch Me 55
   The Best Laid Plans 59
   What Grief Is All About 63
   How Do You Grieve? 65
   Birthdays Will Never Be the Same 69

Chapter 3 A Helping Hand *73*
   The Supportive Role 75
   Surrounded by Widows 77
   What Is Right 81
   How to Help a Mourning Friend 85
   Nourishment 89
   A Soft Place to Fall 91
   The Other Players 93
   Everybody Needs Somebody 97
   Breaching Walls 99

    No Two Ways to Mourn.. 101
    Honoring Lost Loves... 105
    Where Did Everyone Go? 107

Chapter 4 Life Changes 111
    It Takes Patience – Grief Has No Timeline..................... 113
    What Gifts Do You Give a Soul Mate Who Is Gone? 115
    A New Normal.. 119
    You Can Do It … Taking on New Roles 123
    I've Got a Guy for That... 127
    No More Days.. 131

Chapter 5 Signs/Soul Mate Connections......................... 135
    Look for the Quick Hellos 137
    Grieving Beau 139
    Signs or Coincidence?... 145
    The Grandma Book and Messages from Beyond 151
    How Do We Recognize Our Soul Mate? 155

Chapter 6 Healing and Finding Peace............................... 157
    Little Things 159
    The Call that Never Comes 161
    Finding Your Way 165
    Climbing Off the Pity Pot... 167
    Smoothing the Sharp Edges of Grief 171
    Old Spice for Steve 175
    The Courage to Be Happy 179
    Double the Joy 183
    Comfort Where You Find It 187
    What Happened to Peace?... 191
    Choosing Love 193

Epilogue for Dale.. 195

About the Author.. 201

Foreword

During my twenty-five years of trying to help the bereaved on their grief journeys as well as their caregivers, I have come across many wonderful books on grief.

But Cathy Marley's *Breathing Again* is indeed special. It touched me deeply, not only because it contains much wisdom about the grief journey, but also because in it, Cathy shares with us some of her most precious and intimate life experiences.

I will be recommending *Breathing Again* to the

many bereaved I encounter as well as their caregivers as the insights Cathy provides are extremely valuable for all of us on all sides of the grief experience.

Well done and thanks, Cathy, for a most wonderful gift.

Love,

John Chuchman, CDOS, MA, Pastoral Bereavement Educator and Companion

John Chuchman is a man of many facets—pastoral bereavement educator and companion, poet, and author. A gentle soul, he changes lives in the sensitive workshops, seminars, in-service programs, and retreats he regularly offers. And he calms hearts with his wise words in his many books, where he shares his life experiences, spiritual discoveries, frustrations with institutional church, keys to grief healing, as well as his own personal and spiritual growth.

You can reach John, learn more about him, or purchase his books at:
Website: www.sacredtorch.com
Blog: https://sacredtorch.blogspot.com
Books:http://www.sacredtorch.com/index.php/johns-books/

Introduction

I have been very fortunate in my life that I have not encountered the profound grief that comes with the loss of a soul mate. That does not mean I have not had people I love die. I have. My mother when I was twelve years old, my father much later in my life. A step sister. My closest friend in my twenties. Both of my in-laws and any number of people close to me and to my friends. More recently, my son and my soul sister. But never my soul mate. Thank God.

So, is it any wonder that I never really understood how soul-piercing grief can be for someone who experiences that most profound loss of a soul mate? When I first began meeting with my two friends and fellow writers, Joy Collins and Betts McCalla, we called ourselves a book club in that we read other people's work. But it was a book club of very short duration. I quickly discovered that what my two friends needed more than anything was a path to heal the intense grief they felt after the deaths of their soul mate husbands. When we first started meeting, those deaths were still unbearably raw for them both. I did not understand it at the time, but some part of me sensed that they needed a safe place to work through their pain. As we talked and bonded, that safe place ultimately became an endeavor called "From Grief to Peace."

Our goal, we said, was to help others heal their grief and find a measure of peace as they continued on alone in life. We wanted to empower them to overcome that harsh command to "move on" or "get over it." Along the way, my friends began to heal themselves. I saw them begin accepting that while their loved ones are no longer physically here, my friends could make a new life and incorporate them in that new life—not by forgetting them or making them a thing of the past—but by making them part of a new present.

As for me? I learned more than I ever imagined I would about grief. When we first started, I questioned what I could bring to the table. How could I possibly have anything of benefit to say to people who were grieving so deeply? I had no experience. I did not even know what to say and what not to say in the face of grief. They reassured me that I had more to share than I thought. My role, they said, was to serve as the voice of those outside the grief, the friends who wanted to help but felt helpless. Along the way to finding that voice, I learned what they have experienced, what helped them and what hurt. And in seeing how bereft they were on being separated in this lifetime from the loves of their lives, I learned to treasure every moment of the time I have with those I love. I hope that understanding their grief helps ease my own sorrow when, as it is sure to do one day, it comes my way.

Breathing Again is my small effort to speak to the circle of support that surrounds anyone who is mourning the loss of a soul mate. Here, I hope to help you better understand the pain your friend or loved one is experiencing. But most of all, I hope this book will help you be a better friend at a time when your friendship and love are most sorely needed. Although your friend may not be able to ask for your support, perhaps this book will help you know what you can do even if you are not asked.

6 Principles of From Grief to Peace

1. I will allow myself to grieve my soul mate, knowing that this will be hard.
2. I will understand that I have the right to mourn the loss of my soul mate in my own way.
3. I will acknowledge that my grief has no timeline.
4. I will admit that grief has no rules.
5. I will feel comfortable standing up for myself when others put their expectations on me.
6. When I am stronger, I will pay it forward to help others who are mourning the loss of their soul mate.[1]

---

[1] © From Grief to Peace, LLC, 2016, www.FromGriefToPeace.org, reprinted by permission.

Photo by Cathy Marley

Breathing Again

Grief. Sooner or later, death touches us all. And we grieve. You never know when it will come into your life. And unless your heart and emotions are securely padded with bubble wrap, you will one day feel grief's icy touch and mourn to the depths of your soul.

The first time I looked grief in the face, I was twelve. In the course of one unforgettable evening, I went from a carefree young girl looking forward to a summer vacation to a withdrawn, grieving daughter preparing to attend my mother's funeral. I think in some ways, I quit breathing that night. I felt the loss to the depths of my being. But I was not allowed to mourn. I was, after all, just a child. And in those times, everyone believed children could not possibly understand grief. Surely grief is an adult thing. Right? Absolutely not! But I still got the message. And at twelve, I breathed in my sorrow, then held my breath as I carefully encased my emotions in layer after layer of bubble wrap, leaving me numb.

Until very recently, the pain—and yes, anger—that came with my sorrow was still there, protected, intact, unable to reach the essential me. Little did I realize those intense buried feelings of sorrow colored my whole life and kept me from truly feeling anything, or even taking a deep breath.

Almost sixty years later, I am just now learning what it really means to experience a loss of someone you love deeply and to mourn that loss. In all this time, I have managed to remain untouched in the face of death. Relatives and friends have transitioned but because of those bubble-wrapped emotions, I felt little beyond a brief regret that I would never see that person again. And then I went on with my life as though nothing had happened.

But the inevitability of death was waiting in the wings for me to start feeling something. Sure enough, it happened. Thankfully, by then I was better prepared to acknowledge my feelings and understand them as grief.

Breathing Again

It started with two new friends.

I first met Betts and Joy when we were all members of the same writers' group. I met both of their husbands, but while they were married, we never really tried to become close. That started to shift when Betts's husband Jerry passed away. I tried my best to let her know how sorry I was for that loss, although I don't think I was very successful. The best I could do was to meet her for a lunchtime playdate for our dogs. I had no idea of the value that she placed on my visit. To me, that date was more about the dogs than it was about helping a friend who was grieving. Her grief could not penetrate the layers of my personal bubble wrap, so I could not see how shattered she was. I was sympathetic but not particularly empathetic.

And then Joy's husband John died suddenly. Again, I managed to keep my feelings hovering somewhere above her grief. I don't know if I was much help to her, but during one long lunch shortly after his death, I began to see glimmerings of how deeply she was mourning. All I remember doing during that lunch was to let her talk as much as she needed, to listen to her, and to cry with her. Her grief touched something in me, and her loss on top of Betts's loss began to burrow below the layers of bubble wrap.

Some months later, I had what I thought was a brilliant (albeit somewhat self-serving) idea. I wanted to start a book club. I thought of both Joy and Betts mainly because I thought we might enjoy the same books and have some intelligent discussions about them. For them, I think it was a hand of friendship extending into a season of sorrow, but grief and healing never crossed my mind.

Still, the Universe had other ideas. We soon found ourselves talking more about what they had lost and how they were feeling than we talked about books. I think that was meant to be. The talks moved from novels to grief to the idea of writing a book of our own about their experiences with loss. Before we knew it, we had officially picked a name and decided to start a business together, a business about grief. I wasn't sure how I would fit in, but I knew this was important to their healing, and so I went along with them. Our goal was to help others navigate their way through the loss of a soul mate, to avoid all the dead-ends my friends had encountered as they sought ways to find their way through the depths of their own grief. And so, From Grief to Peace was born.

From the beginning, I questioned what I could possibly have to contribute to this incredible effort. After all, I was still blessed with a living husband, a man I love to distraction. My bubble-wrapped emotions denied any other loss, conveniently ignoring my own mother's death when I was so young. Betts and Joy assured me that I brought a unique perspective to what we were doing. Who among us, after all, was better suited to speak for and to those who are outside the immediate grief? We recognized that most people are uncomfortable with death and being close to someone who is consumed by mourning. Thus, they have no idea what to say or what to do, and so they often do the wrong thing.

It has been a learning process for me. My friends have taught me much of what I needed to know. But personal losses after the bubble wrap started to unwind taught me even more. I know it may sound trite and insensitive to someone who has suffered such an agonizing loss as that of a soul mate, but the untimely and far too premature death of a beloved cat ripped away at that bubble wrap and left me emotionally devastated for weeks. I knew there was no comparison to what they had endured, but I began to see glimpses of what my friends were feeling.

And then I lost a soul sister. When Anita died, I knew grief. I really knew grief. Thank God for that earlier, somewhat lesser loss of my cat. It prepared me for this greater, more profound loss. Thank God for all my two friends had taught me about their grief. They prepared me too. Thank God for what they had shown me about life after death. It taught me that love never dies, it just takes on a different, more challenging aspect. I experienced the grief of my loss, but it could not devastate me. I was prepared. And as those I love enfolded me in compassion, I learned what it really means to support someone through a loss.

I am learning that I actually did something right with a single lunch and a doggie playdate all those months ago. It may not have been enough, but it was something. Although I am still uncomfortable with all the feelings that come with grief and showing support to someone immersed in the pain of loss, most of the bubble wrap is gone from my heart now. I can feel their sorrow. I walk in their shoes for at least a few steps. And after all these years, in opening my heart to pain too long suppressed, to feeling the fullness of grief, I am finally beginning to breathe again.

Chapter 1
Is This Really Happening?

Photo by Cathy Marley

What Works for You

The one you love is gone, and suddenly you find yourself alone. In your sorrow, you will be getting advice from every corner of your life, especially for the first few months. *Join a support group ... don't be alone ... get out of the house ... take up a new hobby ... write ... make new friends ... travel ... and so on, and on, and on.* But maybe all you want to do is stay behind the four walls of your home and cry. The last thing you want is people hovering over you. Or maybe you *want* those people around you, lots of them. Yes, you desperately want something to distract you from your grief, but what is the "right" thing?

The fact is, despite all the pain, you are still the same basic person you were before. Your inherent personality has not changed. If anything, it is magnified by tenderness. It is more intensely present and uncensored than ever before. Just being widowed doesn't mean you change who you are and what works best for you. If you were solitary before, you will probably continue to find comfort in being alone. If you were sociable and gregarious, preferring to be with friends before, chances are you will still want people around you now.

There is no right way to do this. Yet, you will find that you need to do *something* once you feel able to take that first step toward overcoming the inertia that enveloped you the moment you realized your love was really gone and you were alone. It is not uncommon to rush from one new "project" or activity to another. Just know that there are things you can do that will fit with your unique personality. Those are the things that will help you the most. They do not have to be complicated or grand in scope. Sometimes the simplest things help the most.

One friend of mine could not stand the thought of going home to her empty house at dinnertime. Instead, she simply walked the extent of her local mall, window-shopping and surrounding herself with life and people, until dinnertime was well past and she could face going home to her empty house. It worked for her because she is very much a people person and always has been.

Another friend flew away to Europe almost immediately after her husband succumbed to his long illness. I know some of you may think it was callous, but the fact is, she had always traveled with her husband, and she was especially adventurous. Traveling was something they loved to do together. Seeing new lands, hearing new tongues, and tasting unfamiliar foods reminded her of the good things they had experienced as a couple. It brought her comfort.

Yet another friend simply could not handle the

stream of well-meaning friends who appeared after her husband's transition. She found her comfort in being alone, meditating, writing, reading, exploring this strange new world she found herself inhabiting. But then, her before world had focused on her relationship with her husband. They were the center of each other's universe, complete in their intimate circle of two. With him gone, she found a new connection with him in the mental and spiritual focus that came in the midst of a familiar solitude. It is a connection that still endures almost six years later.

The thing is, you have to find what works for you in the grief process. You will know what that is because everything else will leave you just a little bit uncomfortable. I'm not saying you should not try new and different things, to step outside your box, if you will. You may discover a new passion you had overlooked before. You may meet new friends who become a lifetime support system. But just recognize that the new things that will last longest are probably the things that fit most closely with who you really are. Those will be the things that work for you.

The Widowed Box

It's just a box on a form—every form. But in that short list of one-word choices is a timeline of your entire adult life. Single. Married. Divorced. Widowed.

The day you move from checking Single to checking Married, you feel a little thrill zing through your heart. You think: *I'm married. I'm really married. And my life is now two, not just me.* It is an exciting moment, filled with potential for a wondrous new way of living. Married is a word of promise and hope, commitment, and beginnings. And if that person is your soul mate, you feel the synergy that comes from your connection. From the very beginning, you know the two of you together are far stronger than either of you has ever been alone. And so it will remain through time. You hope.

For some, the connection may not be as real as you think, and one day you move from checking Married to checking Divorced. The pain you feel from having half your life removed may be a mixture of relief and sadness. But on some level, it is still loss—loss of wonder, loss of promise, loss of your self-image, loss of an imagined future, loss, loss, loss. Suddenly, or perhaps over a too-long time, you are Single again. But now you must still check Divorced, a word of endings and disappointment. There was a time when the world viewed that box like a scarlet letter screaming "failure" to the world. Perhaps in your heart it still feels that way, but checking Divorced is still an acknowledgement that once upon a time, you were part of two, you were married. It took two people to create the divorce, but it still feels intensely personal. And once again you are one.

For the lucky ones, checking Married on the form is a forever thing. You simply know that you will always be part of this pair that came into being when you said, *I do*. You begin checking that box automatically, giving it little thought. It is just the way your life is and will always be. You hope. Until one day, you are alone again through no fault, no divorce, no desired separation. And the day comes when you are faced with one last choice on the list—Widowed. It is a word pregnant with tearful loss, with grief, with solitude.

Until you have to check that Widowed box for the first time, you can never fully understand how traumatic it can be. It's like putting a "finished" stamp on a part of your life that has defined who you are. Joy thought of herself as an integral part of JoyandJohn just as Betts became half of BettsandJerry. Through some mysterious, magical process, they each became more than they had ever been before. And when their soul mates were gone from this life, they both felt that more than half of who they were was gone with them. Of course, both Joy and Betts are strong women. But they will both agree that the absence of the men they knew to be their soul mates has left them somehow less than whole. Although checking that Widowed box made their loss real, it still acknowledged the existence of a relationship that permanently changed who they are.

Joy tells the story of a visit to her broker's office where, shortly after John's death, the secretary had prepared a number of forms for her to sign. For marital status, the woman had thoughtlessly checked Single. Oh, what a vast difference there is between Single and Widowed! It's a lifetime of moments small and great, a shared laugh over a secret joke, hands touching, eyes speaking, hearts connecting. For Joy, checking that Single box represented the ultimate betrayal of her marriage, denying it had ever existed. It was like saying that all the years as an entwined, integral part of JoyandJohn had never happened. A small thing, perhaps, for people who have never been there, but for a woman grieving deeply, it was more painful than having to check the Widowed box. One thoughtless check mark simply erased what she considered to be the best thing that ever happened to her, a connection that made her a far better person, far more than she would have been alone. To her credit, Joy refused to allow that form to negate the years, the rewards, of her marriage. She quietly crossed out Single and checked Widowed. She claimed her widowhood, embracing all the remembered joy and the new pain it represented.

Sadly, that Widowed box is one of the first real-world experiences you face after losing your soul mate. Inevitably, there are forms you must complete for everything. With every form, it rises up and slaps you right in the face, almost shouting, *In the eyes of the world, you are no longer part of two. You are a person alone.*

The first time my friend, Anne, had to check that box after she lost her husband, she went home and cried. She told me, "I felt like a has-been who used to be a wife and was now a disconnected widow. I told myself I was getting old and was being pushed aside, etc., etc. It was a real pity party, but I knew I could not wallow in that self-pity or I would be lost. So, I picked myself up and made myself keep going." Sometimes that is the only way to live with heart-rending grief—allow it, acknowledge the life-changing loss you have suffered, then boot any feelings of self-pity out of your heart, put one foot in front of the other, and just keep slogging ahead. Eventually, momentum will keep you moving forward no matter how much it hurts.

Such experiences are all too common. The fact is that the Widowed box is also something of a badge of honor. Those who check that box know what it is like to be tied at the heartstrings with another human being. And they have survived one of the most grievous losses any of us can experience. But they have survived. They have learned how to keep putting one foot in front of the other, day after day, even when the pain feels unbearable. And they are doing it alone with only sweet memories to sustain them.

Would You Want to Know?

It is a question we have often discussed among ourselves. Is it easier to deal with the sudden death of your soul mate or to have warning and deal with a lingering illness? There are no easy answers.

But what about a combination of the two alternatives? How would you feel if you discovered in their last hours that your soul mate had a terminal illness and had chosen not to tell you that he or she was dying?

Last night I was watching a television program where one main storyline revolved around this issue. Thinking he was protecting his wife, the man who was dying tried his best to keep it from her. Of course, as inevitably happens with such illnesses, his condition worsened to a point where he had to be hospitalized, and he could no longer hide it. Typical of television stories, they quickly reconciled his deception and spent his remaining time in a form of bliss. It felt incredibly false to me. But then, unlike life, it was television where everything is resolved in an hour.

I found myself angry with the character for denying his wife the time she may have needed to come to grips with losing him and to say goodbye properly.

Cathy Marley

Was I wrong to feel that way? Not having personally been through that depth of loss, I don't know. I think that I would have felt a whole gamut of emotions — betrayal, heartbreak, and anger most of all—but I would have also been reluctant to tell him how I truly felt in his final hours. That in itself, I think, would be a form of dishonesty, which has no place in a relationship between soul mates. What a sad legacy to have to carry beyond that ultimate separation. And then once he was gone, I would have still been left to sort through all the feelings. I suspect healing would take forever.

Dying is the one thing we are guaranteed we will have to do alone. No one can do it for us. I wonder what possible benefit could come from choosing to reach that point alone as well? Which is easier for the one left behind? Knowing or not knowing what was coming? Sudden departure or lingering illness? And if in fact there is a lingering illness with no hope of recovery, would you want to know so together you could make the most of the time your loved one has left on this plane? Or would you prefer to have your last days together untainted by the specter of death approaching the door?

Breathing Again

"No matter what, nobody can take away the dances you've already had."
—Gabriel Garcia Marquez

Get Over It? The Constant Weight of Grief

When have you grieved enough? Historically, society dictated when that should happen. Lose a spouse and your wardrobe was expected to go black for at least a year. Gradually, you were allowed to reintroduce color into your world, but only in somber shades. Somehow, a year became the magic number. For a lot of people, that just was not enough. Queen Victoria mourned her Albert for the rest of her days on earth. And she had the power to demand mourning black for everyone in her presence. For Victoria, a lifetime of wearing black and requiring it of those around her was not enough to properly show the depth of her mourning.

Our culture today still allows that year. But over time, it has gradually become less expected. Now, rather than demand you mourn for a year, society expects you to be finished with your grief in that time or less. But what if you are Queen Victoria's modern-day counterpart, and a mere year is simply not enough time to properly mourn a loss that feels as though your very heart has been ripped from your body? *Noooooooooo,* you cry! *I am not ready.* So, what do you do when society pushes you to stop grieving and move on with your life?

Well, you can push back, but the chances are you will be facing accusations of that old psychological bugaboo, "living in denial." I guess you can't really dispute that one without throwing up your hands, giving in to the pressure and declaring, *Hallelujah, I am healed! No more grief. Bring on the dating game.* Now that's probably a lie, right? The fact is, if you have lost a soul mate, you may never be ready for that BS and the grief simply becomes a part of who you are. It integrates. And when asked how you are doing, you learn to put on a happy face and declare, *I'm fine.*

There will probably come a time when someone—most likely your doctor or some well-meaning friend—will declare that you have grieved long enough, slap a depressed label on your psyche, and suggest you turn to antidepressants as a way to "move forward with your life" or worse yet, "get over it." Really? Get over it? Not yet. Not for the love of your life. This is a classic example of how people put their own timelines onto someone else's grieving process. The sad thing is that they are pressing you out of a misguided sense of caring about you. What you may really need is for someone to just listen to you talk, to accept that your life has changed, and to realize you will get over the loss in your own time.

Now, don't get me wrong. For some people,

Breathing Again

antidepressants are a lifesaver. For others, they are little more than a way to short-circuit legitimate feelings that may well be coexisting with some level of happiness—or at least acceptance. The choice should be yours, as is how long you grieve.

Let's face it. You have lost someone who was the center of your world, the other half of your soul, so to speak. You are going to grieve. The profound, unending sorrow may not hit you right away. It takes time, perhaps even into the second year, which is often worse than the first. That is when it hits home with the force of a pile driver that this is really true. Your soul mate is not coming back. And so, you will grieve for as long as you need to. It may last in varying degrees for weeks, months, years, or a lifetime. You will experience peaks and valleys. One day you may wake up and realize the pain is not quite so intense. But in the next moment, you could be instantly reminded of all that is lost and find yourself plunging like a roller-coaster on a downward run to the depths again. Just know this is normal, and not every day will be that way. Some days will be good. Others, not so much.

Some days you will want to climb high up on your self-pity pot and roost there while you give in to feeling intensely sorry for yourself. Yes, you will have bouts of misery where you wonder what you did to deserve being the one left alone. You will want to wail and beat your breast and cry, *Why me?* Your loss has left a huge hole in your heart, and self-pity is a sneaky bastard. It would like nothing more than to take up permanent residence in that gaping hole. You can keep it away, but it will take vigilance and a genuine desire to limit its reach. How? When you feel the "poor me's" coming on, set a timer or an alarm on your computer or cell phone and know that is the time you have to feel sorry for yourself. You determine the time. An hour. Ten minutes. A day. Whatever it is, as long as it is limited. You choose. The time is not what matters. What matters is that in consciously limiting how long you will feel sorry for yourself, you will begin to anticipate living again one moment at a time.

The most serious danger of self-pity is that it is so often rooted in feelings of desperation and can lead you to internal debate over checking out of this life. Please believe me when I tell you that your friends will worry about this, and they do not want to lose you, too. Suicide to follow your departed love is not the answer. This is the time to reach out for a loving hand, a lifeline in the form of a friend, a counselor, or even anti-depressants to help you move through. After you traverse that valley, you will come out the other side and be able to smile without guilt.

In a 2012 speech to families of fallen soldiers, Vice President Joe Biden talked about the constant weight of grief he experienced after losing his wife and daughter in a car crash. He said, "Just when you think, *maybe I'm going to make it*,' you're riding down the road and you pass a field, and you see a flower and it reminds you. Or you hear a tune on the radio. Or you just look up in the night. You know, you think, *maybe I'm not going to make it, man*. Because you feel at that moment the way you felt the day you got the news." He offered a ray of hope, saying, "There will come a day—I promise you, and your parents as well—when the thought of your son or daughter, or your husband or wife, brings a smile to your lips before it brings a tear to your eye. It will happen."

There is no timeline for when you must stop grieving your loss. But at some point, you will begin to move on naturally. That's not to say you will forget the love you have lost. That will be with you for the rest of your life. The grief does not completely go away either; however, in time there will be room for other things. You will begin to live, to breathe, even to laugh again. If you were a healthy, feeling person before, you can be again.

As far as I know, just as there is no timeline for grief, there is no rule book that says you have to stop grieving to keep on living. Shortly after my friend, Anne, lost her husband of thirty-seven years, she told me how grief would overwhelm her without warning. She realized that despite her sorrow, she is basically a happy person and that her happiness and her grief are both part of who she is and who she will always be.

Grief and happiness are not mutually exclusive, and grief can simply be a new thread woven into the warp and woof of the fabric that is your life. If your grief reaches the point of coloring the entire tapestry, then by all means, you may find that an antidepressant can help you put it back into its proper perspective. However you choose to handle your grief, the fact is that it is now a part of you. As you move forward, the

Cathy Marley

day will come when you can remember a joke your loved one would say, and smiling as you remember how good it was, you will enjoy the memory. In time, you will find that the good memories and the joys will be the ones that sustain you, and the grief of loss will fade gradually into the background. That is an entirely new fabric of your life. That new fabric, colored as it is by both happiness and sorrow, will be richer in texture and closer to your heart.

Breathing Again

Oh, I Get by with a Little Help ...

Most of my life, I have been pretty self-sufficient. Okay, make that independent, VERY independent. Asking for help has always been my last possible option, never the first. Well, the Universe finally slapped me upside the head and said, "We're going to teach you a lesson about asking for and graciously accepting a little help. LEARN this lesson!"

On a hot Tuesday evening in August, Norm and I were in an automobile accident. It could have been worse, but it was bad enough. Fortunately for old "I can do it myself" me, Norm came through with nothing more serious than a badly bruised sternum. I ended up with a broken wrist. That meant I needed him. I really needed him. It is mind-boggling how much we rely on two functional hands. I certainly gained a new respect for anyone who goes through life with any handicap. I insisted on trying to write and keep powering ahead with all the projects I was working on, but my typing speed had dropped from "pretty darned fast touch typing" to a one-handed snail's pace as I visually sought out every letter. It was a nightmare for a professional writer!

But I did learn the lesson: Ask for help when you

need it! Friends and family all stepped forward and offered to help. Saying no only made life more difficult. Saying yes gave me a new appreciation for the generosity that lies in other hearts. The night of the accident, dear Betts offered to drive us to the ER and wait with us. I stubbornly turned her down. After all, I wasn't positive that wrist was broken, was I? Crazy thinking told me I could handle whatever I needed to do the next day on my own without "inconveniencing" a friend. We ended up spending most of that next day in the ER after all—without the comfort of a friend to hold our hands.

Still, it is a giant leap from accepting help when it is offered to actually asking for it. Pain and immobility taught me to ask. I asked for rides. I asked Norm to drive me to appointments even though he had almost quit driving. I asked him to cook and wash dishes, and he did without complaint. I asked our daughter and daughter-in-law for help. They came the next day, doing whatever they could to get us through the next week, including bringing several home-cooked meals. And, when our new kitten ran outside, I took the ultimate risk and called my neighbor at 10 p.m. to help us catch him. Within minutes, she had him safely back inside.

Just being even marginally incapacitated (and yes, in the grand scheme of things, a broken wrist is marginal), I learned that, as the Beatles song says, *I can get by with a little help from my friends*. I can't imagine having to go through something like the aftermath of our accident alone, and yet, those who have lost a mate do it every day, and somehow they manage. It must be an overwhelmingly frightening and lonely experience for them. I can only hope they can learn, as I did, to ask for help. When you are hurt—or grieving—and in need, people want to help. You might even say it is a gift to them when you accept their offer, even more so when you ask for it. Asking says you trust them enough to let that vulnerability show. There is no shame in asking, only strength and comfort gained in knowing you are loved and valued.

Chapter 2
How You Feel

Photo by Cathy Marley

Walls – Protection or Prison?

I think grief can gladly hide behind walls, walls of remembrance, walls of solitude, walls of *I'm fine*. The more impenetrable the wall, the stronger the protection for an aching heart. And so, we build strong walls to contain our mourning. Hiding there can feel safe. At first.

We build our walls to keep us safe from a world suddenly unfamiliar, but we forget that they also keep us inside their boundaries. Walls are more than protection. They can become prisons, prisons so high and strong that we see no way out. Those are the walls that must be conquered as you heal and find your way to peace.

What kind of walls have you built to contain your grief?

Know there are some out here who have faith in your innate strength, who know you can surmount the walls you have built. You are not alone. We want to help. Start climbing. Those of us who love you and mourn alongside you are waiting on the other side with

Cathy Marley

loving arms stretched wide, just waiting to enfold you in love. We are sending strength your way as you topple the walls that no longer need to be your prison.

Strong

A fog clad wall
Rises before me,
Its misty top
Beyond view.

I blow
But the wall remains.

I push
But the wall remains.

I *wish* it gone
But the wall remains.

I paint it bright
But the wall remains.

I cry for help.
Still the wall stands,
Tall, forbidding.

Slumped
Against the wall,
I feel a stone.

Breathing Again

My fingers rise
And find another.

Arms reach,
Muscles flex.
I pull
And climb.

At the top,
I triumph and
The useless wall falls.

It is weak.
I am strong.
I will prevail.

Breathing Again

I'm Fine

"Hey, I'm tougher than I look," I confidently informed the orthopedic surgeon as he pulled the needle from my knee. Sometimes that's true, but this time it was just so much braggadocio. Okay, it was pure, unadulterated BS. I can usually handle just about anything you can throw at me and not blink—until no one is watching. I managed it this time, too—barely. By the time I limped my way to the car after the injection into my knee, I was lightheaded, sweating, and gasping for breath. My knee felt like someone had stuffed a football into it. I collapsed into the car and just sat there for a while trying to regain my equilibrium enough to turn the key and drive home. Yes, my superwoman ego had insisted I was perfectly capable of driving myself home alone. Once there, I collapsed for the rest of the day. I guess I am not as tough as I think, as tough as I try to convince everyone else I am, as fine as I claim.

Perhaps that is the plight of strong, independent women. I'm not the only one I know who is like that. The girlfriends I surround myself with are all like that. Ask how they are doing and their automatic response is invariably, *I'm fine*. Not having talked to her in several months, I once asked my sister how she was doing and she followed the *I'm fine* with an oh-by-the-way story of how she had recently broken her hip, and convincing herself she was just bruised, waited more than a week to see a doctor. It was the same reply Joy choked out through tears on the anniversary of her husband's death. And ask me how I'm doing when I am fresh out of surgery and stumbling around in a drug-induced haze, and you will probably also hear me say, "I'm fine. That wasn't as bad as I thought it would be."

Sometimes it *is* as bad as we thought it would be. Sometimes, it is worse and *I'm fine* hides the worst pain you have ever known. When mourning colors your every moment, and others keep asking how you are, false declarations that you are fine may well be little more than a ploy to deflect those well-meaning questions. Declaring yourself to be just fine and dandy simply becomes a way of stopping them from interfering with your grief. After a while—that socially acceptable interval after which people begin to think you *should* be getting over the loss of the one you loved more deeply than life—you begin to feel that talking about the pain you are living with becomes more of a burden to others than a balm to yourself. And so, you begin to declare yourself *fine*. And perhaps, on some level deep in your mind you think you can fake it till you make it. Maybe, just maybe if you say it often enough, it will someday be true.

Those who cannot see through the lie are placated and drift away to go on with their busy lives, believing that you really are just fine. But if we listen hard enough, if we listen through a filter of love, we can hear the self-protective lie that paints the words like a thin scab covering a festering wound. The words are easily pierced, and the pain can be freed. That is when our job is to simply follow up with a deeper question and ask, "I know you say you're fine, but how are you *really* doing?" Our purpose then is to listen to you, to let you know that however you are really doing is okay, and to lovingly open the way for you to honestly tell us what is going on with you when you are really not doing fine at all.

Breathing Again

The Ka-thunk

No matter what your life is like, routine eventually finds its way into your world. It's only human to be a creature of habit, and so we go through life in a way that rarely takes much thought. Everyone's routine is different. Some are smooth and unhurried. Others are more chaotic. But we all have one. You get up in the morning, brush your teeth, shower, eat breakfast, and move on with your day. Night comes and the bedtime routine rarely varies. Most days, life tends to roll along smoothly. Oh, there are sometimes bumps in the road, but they are generally pretty predictable and reasonably well-balanced. The smooth road, the mesmerizing hum of a predictable routine, is the one we all prefer. It just makes life a little easier.

And when there is a soul mate there beside you, the routine becomes something of a graceful, carefully choreographed dance. Like planet and moon of equal size, you revolve around each other, your place in the heavens defined by his, his by yours. Even when you are miles and miles apart, you each feel the gravitational pull of the other. You simply know that loved one is out there—somewhere. Until, one day, they aren't.

I once watched an episode of the comedy *Two*

and a Half Men on television where two of the main characters were talking about predictable routines as they moved around the kitchen early in the morning. Both denied they followed any routine, insisting every day was fully spontaneous from morning to night. And yet, throughout the entire scene, they stepped around one another without looking. Routine ruled. One moved through the steps of preparing their coffee, fully focused on coffee, water, coffeemaker, cups, while the other made toast and moved from bread box to toaster to refrigerator to cabinet—all with his nose buried blindly in a newspaper. Never once was there a misstep, never once as much as an accidental brush against one another. You could almost hear waltz music playing in the background. Living with your soul mate is a lot like that.

Losing a soul mate disturbs that natural balance of your existence. You may find yourself dancing around an invisible partner, following the same steps your body knows to follow through long years of habit. But the routine, while familiar, seems somehow vaguely wrong.

The loss leaves you somewhat like a cart with a bad wobbly wheel, always just a little bit off from the rest of the world and strangely out of balance. You can go along every day knowing you are not totally in sync and still function just fine. But lurking somewhere in the back of your mind is the awareness that the flat spot is there. Then one day, one hour, the flat side finds its way yet again to the bottom of your wheels and life, with a silent *ka-thunk*, hits a bump. Your heart clenches with grief as you are reminded of what is missing in your routines, and you are hit yet again with the imbalance that is an integral part of who you have become.

You never know when that wheel will hit the flat side, but when it does, you are forcibly reminded once again that things are just not quite right. At that moment, all you can do is keep pushing ahead until your cart starts rolling smoothly again, and then let yourself roll ahead until the next bump hits. And it will. You see, the bumps are not out there. They are in your heart, and only you know when something has found them. Only you can move forward or steer around them.

Do I Still Matter?

In the movie *South Pacific*, the heroic French plantation owner Emile, sees nurse Nellie Forbush across a room and is instantly enchanted. Their song, "Some Enchanted Evening," speaks of the magic that happens when soul mates find one another. In it, he sings of the magnetic pull that draws soul mates together, an irresistible, instinctive attraction that compels you to fly across a crowded room to make that person your own.

Finding your soul mate is the moment you know you are complete. Life up to that point has been shadowed by a vague feeling that somehow a part of you is missing, but when you meet that love, the recognition is undeniable. Your world shifts and from that moment on, you know you belong, you matter to that one person. As that person does to you. Like twin moons, you orbit around the single world that is your relationship.

Your identity can so easily become one. It just feels natural to be, as we all have been in our lives, NormandCathy or JerryandBetts or JohnandJoy. Inseparable. Complete in one another to the extent that the rest of the world could easily become extraneous.

Lose half of the equation and you may not be sure how to be just yourself.

Joy says it so eloquently, "No one *gets* us like our partners do. No one lives and breathes us like we do for each other. We were always in each other's thoughts and my every moment—waking and sleeping—was connected to John. We carried each other with us as we went about our day, and I knew that wherever I was and whatever I was doing, John was there in the world with me. It was more than need although that was comforting. Rather, it was that he was my safe place to land. He was *Home*."

When your life is so deeply entwined with another, losing that person leaves you in a foreign land, unable to speak the language and ignorant of the customs and what is expected of you. Fear becomes a familiar companion. Fear of being alone. Fear of the sorrow lurking on the fringes of every waking moment. Fear that you will disappear and no one will notice.

You begin to realize all the day-to-day things you are missing. You become touch-starved, craving the smallest hug or gentle touch on the arm. You miss having someone to simply say, *you look great, babe.* The little rituals, the kiss hello, the goodbye wave, all the little pieces that wove the tapestry of your life are gone. And you suddenly realize how important he or she was when you really had not given them much thought *before.* No longer are you the center of someone's life. No one's face lights up to see you when you come home—just the dog, but dogs are always excited to see you. All the things that say you are important to someone, that you are well loved, are lost. And you ask yourself, *Do I even exist or have I become little more than a ghost ship cut adrift from my anchor in this world? Do I still matter?*

The answer is yes. You do still matter. You do still exist. There are those of us who still treasure you, and we are still here. You matter to us. Our relationship is, undoubtedly, a totally different, less intense one than the one you have lost. But it is a relationship nonetheless, and it can grow. It can provide you with a new place to anchor. It may not be as deep or as secure as the anchorage you have lost; however, it can give you a safe harbor now when you need one the most.

As time passes, you will find that you begin to adapt. You will never forget the one who was always the *home* you sought in a storm. No one who loves you would expect you to. Seeing you heal and being a small part of that healing, however long it takes, is a gift I know I would treasure. It would deeply enrich my life, as do you. And it is a gift only you can give. So yes, you do still matter.

Touch Me

I once asked a friend what she missed most after her husband died. Her answer surprised me. "Touch," she said. "I miss being touched." The sadness and isolation in her voice were palpable, and I wanted to cry for her. Instead, I reached out and enfolded her in a deep, heart hug.

How often, I thought, do we wrap ourselves in a lonely bubble, its outer perimeter ever rebounding off the bubbles of those around us? We can clearly see the grieving or lonely or needful person beside us, and yet it is so easy to just bounce away without reaching out to make a very human connection. And the need is there. Oh, how ever present is our need to be touched! For the person who is grieving, that sympathetic touch and a genuine question, *How are you doing, how are you REALLY doing?* may be all that is needed to unleash a flood of tears. Unshed, they have kept a heart bound and aching, but your simple, honestly caring question opened the floodgates.

Serving as both shield and mask, our skin is so much more than a simple barrier. It protects all that we have inside, shielding our delicate inner body and masking so much of our vulnerable psychic selves that we choose to hide. No matter how tough we try to be, its thousands of nerve endings still connect us to the outside. Through touch, we can stir fiery demons, soothe their painful fires, or just simply connect with another human being.

Research has shown that of our five senses, touch is perhaps the most essential and most neglected. Sometimes called skin hunger, touch deprivation can affect our well-being, regardless of age. It is a proven fact that babies need human contact to thrive, patients who are touched often heal more quickly, and elderly people who receive even the smallest touches are often noticeably healthier than those who do not. Even snuggling with a warm, soft cat or dog can satisfy that need for contact and help us feel accepted and whole. I'm not saying we need to run around mauling each other or even engaging in huge full-body hugs with every person we meet. But a gentle pat on the arm or a compassionate hug to connect human to human goes miles toward reassuring others that they are not alone on this planet.

My friend Joy tells a story of working with premature babies. One in particular has stayed with her for years. Born very early, he had been confined to an incubator for the first weeks of his little life and had been fed via a feeding tube. He always seemed to be tense, cranky, and restless. Finally, the day came when Joy was asked to give him his first bottle feeding. She carefully swaddled the squirming, mewling infant in a soft blanket, picked him up, and cuddled him. It was his first human contact. Before she could even start to feed

Breathing Again

him the bottle, he relaxed and quieted, closing his eyes in blissful contentment. Just that one touch, that's all it took.

Too many of us go through our days wrapped in isolation, rarely reaching out or inviting contact. What a lonely existence that can be! I can only imagine how much lonelier it is for someone who has known and lost the intimacy of a soul mate. In a marriage or any intimate relationship, every day is filled with those small rituals and gestures that come in the form of a brief hug or a kiss, an inside joke, a special toast over wine, a touch on the arm, a warm and loving body in bed beside you, or a myriad of other small unconscious moments of reaching out. Take that person away and it is as though there is suddenly a void there each time you reach out to connect. The hand you instinctively reach to hold is gone. Where there was once a familiar aura drawing you like a magnet, there is nothing, and that side of your energy seems to fray away into empty space. It is as though you have forgotten to eat for far too long and suddenly realize hunger is permeating your very being. Your skin is starving. You may attribute the feeling to grief and that may well be a huge part of it, but your body, your psyche is craving the smallest hug or gentle touch on the arm. It needs connection. It needs to feel the food of touch.

As a friend, I know words alone cannot really ease the pain of grief. They are, after all, only words, nothing more. But I can reach out in even more basic ways. I can start with the most profound touch I have at my command. I can hug. Not just the pat on the back, mommy hug, or the fraternal stiff teepee hug, but the true heart-to-heart hug. Nothing can replace that for making a connection that transcends isolation. The beat of one heart crosses barriers of flesh and bone to connect with another and truly convey what nothing else can. It is not just a hug. It is the most profound expression of love I can give. I can only hope that the strength and peace that beat within my heart can find its way to the heart of my grieving friend through a hug.

Breathing Again

"Life is what happens to you while you're busy making other plans."
— *John Lennon*

"Man plans, God laughs."
— *Yiddish proverb*

The Best Laid Plans ...

I'm a planner. The busier I am, the more I plan. But lately I am discovering that sometimes my best laid plans can go flying out the window in a heartbeat. Life, in all its unpredictability, happens when it chooses to, not when my plans say it should.

Last weekend, after fifty-two long days in the body shop, my car was finally repaired following the accident I had in early August. That accident was the start of a full cycle of life happening despite my careful planning. Saturday was like a day of dominoes lined up in a row tumbling one into the other. Life happening kicked into high gear.

In the same month as the accident, the car's registration expired. Now, I am almost obsessive about paying that type of bill on time (I really do not like late fees), but this time I could not send in the payment. You see, the car needed an emissions test, and because it was in the shop, the test was impossible to do. Life happening again.

I rolled with the punches and purchased a waiver that gave me three days to take the car straight from the repair shop to the testing station. Not wanting a ticket for expired registration, I did just that. I picked the car up at 8 a.m. on Saturday morning and drove directly to have it tested. And again, life happened to derail my plans for a speedy test and registration.

The technician plugged everything in and almost immediately unplugged it again. He then announced that my car was not ready. "Not ready?" I asked. "What does that mean?" As it turns out, it meant I had not completed a *drive cycle* after having the car's computer and battery disconnected for so long. Fifty-two days, remember? Aaaannnnd, life happening number three.

Now, a drive cycle, apparently varies from car to car, and no one at the testing station could tell me what it is for my car. Life happening number four? Maybe a mini one.

After calling the dealer, I discovered a drive cycle for my car involves warming the engine at idle from fully cold until it reaches normal operating temperature and then driving at freeway speeds for at least fifteen minutes. Easy. Except for the start out cold part. My car was already nice and hot, so even though I had a long freeway drive to make that day, it wouldn't count. Drive cycle postponed to Sunday. Life happening number five?

Breathing Again

Well, I finally managed to pass the emissions test and pay for the registration (with a late fee) by Monday afternoon, after two rounds of long, aimless driving.

My point is that I had planned my Saturday and the whole registration renewal carefully. I needed to, since I knew the week ahead was going to be a very busy one with little opportunity to add anything extra. But life intervened and derailed much of that plan. At every turn, I had to adapt to a new obstacle thrown before me.

Foolishly, I kept thinking, *Things could not get any worse.* But a little voice in my head said, *Oh yes they could. Be careful what you think.* And then life happened and something new and challenging popped up like a jack in the box, gleefully shouting, *Surprise!* Nothing was ever catastrophic, but just enough happened to keep reminding me to be grateful for how minor each event was in the grand scheme of things. With each new challenge, I struggled to maintain my perspective and remember the *at leasts*. At least the car was repairable. At least I finally had it back. At least it seemed as good as new. At least the accident wasn't my fault. At least our injuries were healing, and we would recover in time. And most importantly of all, at least neither of us was hospitalized or killed.

Which brings me full circle back to what From Grief to Peace is all about.

I know losing a soul mate is one of the most painful events anyone can ever experience. The loss of

Cathy Marley

someone so intimately connected to you is like a physical rending of your very soul. No one can come through that unscathed. And when you think of all the wonderful plans you had for the rest of your life together, it is doubly difficult. To paraphrase John Lennon, you made plans but life had a different idea.

I would like to think that perhaps some of the *at leasts* can help you, the survivor, endure until you can be reconnected. At least you found each other. At least you had precious time together. At least you had love. At least you will be together again.

Breathing Again

What Grief Is All About

I'm a little bit old-fashioned. Every morning over coffee, I read the newspaper—yes, the print version—from front to back. Every day, I see any number of obituaries, and I have reached an age where I scan those listings looking for familiar names. I am always a little relieved when I don't find anyone I know there.

I suppose most of the people in those obituary listings did not expect to die that day. Nor did their loved ones expect to lose someone they loved on that specific day. I think death catches everyone unprepared, some more so than others. None of us is ever completely ready to die or to lose someone we love, even when long illness has set the stage.

This morning, I got to thinking about those people who are listed there. Some of them have long, very descriptive obituaries, a testament written by those left behind, if you will, to a full life. Others are little more than three lines sometimes asking for anyone who knew them to come forward. How very sad. I know that at some point in their life, those lonely people were happy children, hopeful teens, increasingly disillusioned adults. Somewhere along the way, they lost purpose and never found it again. Until one day, death found them. I would like to believe that after transitioning, they were able to see some impact they made on this world.

    I believe that when we mourn, what we are really mourning is the loss of a life that impressed itself upon our heart. Each person who touches us in one way or another in our lifetime leaves a mark. Some of those connections are brief, and the marks they leave are relatively superficial. Others, like our soul mates, are so deeply imbedded in our very soul that losing them is very much akin to major surgery. The scar left from the loss is both deep and permanent. We never return to the shape we were before they came into our life. The impact they have made on the world and on us is immeasurable, and we memorialize and mourn the end of that impact. And when all is said and done, isn't that what grief is all about?

Photo by Cathy Marley

How Do You Grieve?

    Once upon a time, there were three of us. Now, there are only two. We were best friends, soul sisters I think, and even though one of us lived miles and miles away, we still felt the connection. Once or twice a year, usually at least for Christmas and maybe a birthday, we would meet and it always felt as though no time had passed. We easily picked up where we had left off, but we took the time in between for granted. I took it for granted, anyway.

When Anita died, I discovered some things very important about myself. It took a while and it took Elaine, my remaining soul sister from our triad, to make me look at how I handle grief.

At first, I immersed myself in the short-term tasks, busy work if you will. I offered to host a Celebration of Life. I made a music playlist. I wrote lists and shopped for food. All that activity made for a very nice excuse to distance myself from concerned friends and family, from life itself. I was very busy on a most important task, after all. I did not realize that distancing had become a comfortable habit. I did not realize how deeply I was burying my grief in frenetic *doing* rather than allowing myself to feel or ask for help.

For some reason I still don't completely understand, I distanced myself from Elaine more than anyone else. Despite my best intentions, I didn't call or e-mail. I even managed to conveniently ignore texts, the ultimate form of immediate communication. And I stopped really talking about Anita. I wasn't denying the fact of her death. I think I just did not want to face the emotions it brought up in me. And perhaps I stepped away from Elaine because the reminder of what we had both lost was just too painful. Numbness was easier but only in the immediate moment.

I realized how much I was hurting not only Elaine but myself when she told me that in not hearing from me, she felt like she had lost two friends. Comfort can lie in others if we allow them in, but I was not doing that. Instead, I was retreating into isolation. That had never worked before, nor has it this time. The sadness is still there, and it will be always.

I learned that I handle my grief alone and in silence. I may appear strong and in control, but inside, my heart is screaming. I never fall apart in front of anyone. Rather, I may come across as a stoic rock. It may not be the healthiest way to deal with the feelings, but it is me. I'm not sure I can change, but for one baby step at a time I plan to give it a try. I have also learned four things about grief that perhaps can help others, people like you.

- When you are grieving, sometimes your body keeps moving because it has to, but your mind and heart are far away, disconnected from what is going on around you. There is nothing wrong with this, it just is.
- Withdrawing may feel like it will help, and maybe it does for a while, but sometimes opening yourself to outside help from someone who cares, even if only for whatever moment you can handle, may be a healthier choice.
- Your grief may be all you can see, but hopefully you will one day look up and see those around you who are also grieving. Mourning and remembering together may help make it easier for you both.
- Reaching out to help someone else who is grieving deeply can be healing for you. There can be comfort in clinging to one another.

Breathing Again

Photo by Circus Vargas

Birthdays Will Never Be the Same

As I approach my birthday this month, I realize that it will be my first one since losing my dear friend and soul sister, Anita. Make no mistake. I am grateful to still have the comfort of family and other friends, and I am sure we will celebrate in one way or another, but this birthday will still not be the same without her in this world.

I could always look forward to her phone call, her lovely cards, and the most thoughtful gifts a girlfriend could ever want. Last year, for my seventieth birthday, she made the long journey from Oregon just to celebrate a major milestone with me. What a lovely celebration we had! Anita, Elaine, and I had a delightful dinner, and then we topped it off with a night at the circus. Oh my! There were acrobats and clowns and magicians and aerial acts, and all the wonderful things that make a circus magical even for those of us who are only young at heart.

For as long I live, I will treasure the memory of that night and the photo of the three of us best friends smiling at the sheer joy of that last magical evening together. We had no idea of what the near future held for us, that only Elaine and I would be celebrating her sixtieth birthday this year or that we would not be able to see Anita on her seventieth in August.

After Christmas, we had one last day together. We had chosen to celebrate those three pivotal birthdays together with a road trip to the arts community of Tubac for browsing, shopping, eating, and just simply spending time together. I thank God for that January day and the quality time it gave us. In February, Anita was gone, leaving us to face all the rest of our birthdays without her. Now we are left with just sweet memories flavored with a touch of sorrow for what will never be again.

I find myself understanding how grief can walk hand in hand with regret. And I want to remind others to savor every moment of the here and now. Store memories like precious gems. And if you have lost a soul mate or, as I have, a soul sister, open your treasure chest whenever you are grieving and find solace in the riches you have stored within.

Chapter 3
A Helping Hand

Photo by Cathy Marley

The Supportive Role

The supportive role of friend to someone who has lost their soul mate is not always an easy one, but when it is founded on love, it becomes patient and kind and unselfish, and most of all, non-judgmental.

I cannot pretend to know what it feels like to lose my soul mate. I do have friends who have been there and I try to understand, to be as supportive as I can. I do not always succeed in helping them live with their grief, but I do try. I try to suspend my life for the few minutes it takes to call and just touch base, to ask how they are doing, how they are REALLY doing. And then instead of trying to think of what I am going to say or how to avoid causing them more pain, to listen, really listen to what they say, to engage with them. I try to remember birthdays and anniversaries, both happy ones and sad, because I know they will be especially tender and vulnerable on those days. I try to step out of my own confining little box of routine and remember to include them in my life, asking them to dinner, a movie, shopping, or simply coffee for an hour. If they are up to it, I am thrilled. If not, I hold on to accepting where they are. They deserve a pass for as long as they need it. They are mourning. I am not. That is all the reason I need.

Surrounded by Widows

I have reached a point in life where I find myself surrounded by widows instead of new brides. In less than a year, four friends have lost their husbands, the latest just yesterday. And two of my closest friends, Joy and Betts, are still grieving their husbands' deaths years after the loss. Decades after their husbands moved much too soon to the next plane, I know my daughter and my sister still mourn those untimely deaths. To this day, they can tear up when they think of the husbands they lost. I suppose they always will.

I love all these women and wish I knew what to do to ease their sorrow. I don't. Even though I have spent hours talking with Joy and Betts about the loss of a mate, I still don't really know what to do, how to help soothe their broken hearts. Perhaps my uncertainty contains an element of discomfort on my part and desire to distance myself from such deep grief. Frankly, my response to their loss frightens me. On too many levels, it frightens me.

I must be honest here. When a friend's husband or significant partner dies, leaving behind a devastated woman with a hole in her heart, I immediately personalize the loss. I suppose it is only human, but it still feels so very selfish. Are all these losses for my friends a warning from the Universe that I should prepare myself to be alone? That one thought leaves me worrying about how much time I have left with my Norm and wanting desperately to protect him and keep him well. I want to throw my arms around him and demand he stay with me. But I know that is unrealistic and not possible. I find myself, instead, pleading with the Universe to let me go first so I can avoid the pain I know lies along that solitary road without him. But that, too, is outside my control.

I imagine myself inside my friends' skins and wonder what they are feeling. I can only imagine their pain. I have not been there, but I can see the pain etched on their faces, the deep sadness in their eyes. What if it was me? How would I cope? *Could* I cope, or would I fall apart? I think I would probably be stoic. That is, after all, how I handle a lot of things in life. But inside, I would be wailing and screaming, beating my breast in grief. Is this how my friends are dealing with their losses? To varying degrees, they all seem numb to me. Perhaps that is a mechanism we turn to in order to keep our hearts from shattering, to help us keep putting one foot in front of the other even when we cannot feel the ground beneath us.

When I learn of these losses, I try to do all the right things. I attend the services or celebrations of life. I send cards and I donate to the chosen charity or I send flowers, but it never feels like enough. It isn't. The widow needs more than the immediate, token gestures made at the peak of my awareness. All too often, I fail

Breathing Again

in the follow-up. I wake up one day and realize that weeks have passed while I got on with the busyness of my life. I have thought about my friend—often. But I have not acted on those thoughts nearly enough. I often allow myself to fall into the trap of thinking that waiting to call is better. I think I delude myself with that thought.

In the meantime, my friend is simply trying her best to soldier on. Weeks that have gone far too fast for me have felt like years to her. At the beginning, a new widow is surrounded by attentive friends and family. Sometimes even that is too much for her. She wants people but not every waking moment. Often, they are there when she simply needs to be alone to cry and let her guard down. But one at a time all those people drift away, and inevitably the widow is left alone. That is when she needs people the most. My problem is in identifying that turning point and knowing when to be there.

I remember Betts talking about the difficult times after Jerry died. She said the dinner hour was always the hardest. That had always been their special time, and she simply could not bring herself to go home to her empty house and an end-of-the-day mealtime without him. Rather, after work she would go to the mall where she could be in crowds of people but not with them. There, she would wander aimlessly and window-shop and wander some more for hours until dinnertime had passed. Then she could face going home to her quiet, empty house. She told me that she craved being with someone who would talk to her about Jerry and the good times they had together. All too often, people avoided even mentioning him for fear of hurting her. She needed to hear his name and know he was not completely erased from their world. Sometimes, she simply wanted someone to sit with her, eating popcorn and watching movies on television. It wasn't about being entertained. It was more about the simple, undemanding presence of another human being sharing the same space with her. That is what I struggle with learning how to do.

So much of how we deal with grieving has to do with our own personal discomfort and fears. We want to kiss the boo-boo and make it all better once and for all, but we cannot. Losing a great love is infinitely more than just a boo-boo and we know it. We feel bad for our friend, and that is okay. It is normal for any caring person, but we cannot make it better for them. All we can do is meet them where they are, be there to listen— or not—as they need, and let them be okay with their grief. My friends are showing me how to do that. It is not easy, and I may not always do it well. But it is the best way I can be a friend to them as they learn to accept their loss as an integral part of the rest of their life, one that colors every moment and new experience. One conversation about the loved one who is gone, one hug, one phone call, one lunch or dinner at a time, I can do small things that may make a huge difference in the bleak days of a grieving friend. It is the least I can do in the name of love.

What Is Right

I am grieving today. But despite my grief, I am also trying to support others who are mourning the loss of my friend—her brother, his whole family, our other soul-sister, her many friends from around the world. All of our hearts are breaking in one way or another.

Suddenly I get it. As hard as I have tried to learn what to say or what to do, I still really don't know what is *right*. I think *right* depends on the person. For some, it is simply putting your arms around one another and allowing the tears to fall. For others, it's a card or flowers or food. Sometimes it's as simple as saying a heartfelt, "I am so sorry for your loss, for *our* loss." I guess I forget that last one all too often. It seems to be such a staple phrase on television police dramas that it somehow feels a little trite and overused. But said with heart, it is truly the sincerest and most personal expression of sympathy. And I find myself saying it because I am learning that it is far gentler than offering unsolicited advice. And it does comfort.

In From Grief to Peace, we established six principles that we believe can give you a foundation for dealing with the often insensitive onslaught of the outside world during those first days of grief and find your way to a peace that will allow you to go on with life. The sixth principle says, *When I am stronger, I will pay it forward to help others who are mourning the loss of their soul mate.*[1] If I can pay anything forward to those who so want to help, it is to remind them that sometimes the kindest thing you can do is to offer yourself, to be present, to be mindful of the person who is mourning, and offer not advice but what is right for that individual. It is what others are doing for me as I mourn my friend. It is what I try to do for them as they, too, mourn.

[1] © From Grief to Peace, LLC, 2016, www.FromGriefToPeace.org, reprinted by permission

Meet Me Here

I know you want
To help,
But only I can
Shed these tears.

I know you want
To soothe,
But only I can
Know this broken heart.

I know you hurt
For me, for you.
Let me be okay
With the grief.

Meet me where I am,
Help me with …
… a kind word
… a gentle touch
… a fond memory
… your open heart.

Breathing Again

How to Help a Mourning Friend

    I always feel incredibly powerless in the face of grief. I never know if I am saying or doing the right thing. But my friends have taught me that doing something is so much better than doing nothing or ignoring their sorrow. The death happened. There is no getting around that terrible fact. They are grieving. That is a fact as well and not to be denied. So, I have listened to my friends as they talked about what they needed and what they still need. I think anything we can do to help must be based on these things: honesty, compassion, empathy, presence.

    Stay in touch. In the early days after a loss, those who are left behind are surrounded with friends and family. All of them want to help ease the grief. As time goes along, however, people forget or life reasserts itself, and they begin to drift away. That is when the loneliness can set in, and the hard finality of loss becomes unavoidable. You may well be needed more in the second year than in the earliest days. Staying in touch sends out a lifeline that says, *I still care and will be with you for however long you need someone.*

    1. Call just to say, "Hello, how are you doing, how are you *really* doing?" Do this often, not just

once. It may take many tries before your friend gets the message that you really want to know.
2. E-mail, Facebook, and texting are brief ways to say you are thinking about that person without added pressure.
3. Share your latest good read with your friend and offer to discuss it when he or she finishes.

Include them. In a world of couples, it is all too easy to forget about those who are no longer part of a pair. The solitude that comes with that new existence can be devastating. Like little Kevin in the movie *Home Alone*, the one left alone may feel he or she is standing outside the window looking in at the rest of the world enjoying companionship and special occasions. Just know that your friend may not always be up to accepting your invitations, but they will always appreciate your thoughtfulness.
1. Invite your friend to see the latest comedy or blockbuster hit with you.
2. Invite him or her to join you for dinner. If that is too much, maybe breakfast or a coffee date.
3. Remember that holidays can be especially difficult. Include your friend in Christmas dinner, Thanksgiving, family parties and picnics, and so forth.

Offer distractions. Release any expectations. Sometimes all your friend needs is to simply have another living being there, so he or she is not alone. Just know that your friend may not welcome distractions right away, but one day they will.

Breathing Again

1. Make a date to watch a video and eat popcorn together. Bring the popcorn. Wine is optional but probably a great idea. Talking is optional, too. Bonus points for watching a movie your friend enjoyed together with his or her lost loved one.
2. If they like pets but are currently petless, offer to have a playdate to share your fur babies. If your friend does have pets, plan a playdate for the pets.
3. Consider taking a short class or attending a lecture as an opportunity to spend time together.

Keep the memories alive. You can be sure it hurts more to act as though the lost loved one has been erased than it is to talk about him or her. The lost loved one is still very much alive in your friend's heart. Anyone who is living with grief needs to know they are not alone in their memories.

1. Reminisce about the times you had together with your friend's lost loved one.
2. Encourage your friend to talk about the lost loved one and what he or she is feeling. And LISTEN!
3. Call the loved one by name. It keeps that person's memory alive in a good way.
4. Write a note to your friend recalling one special memory of the one they have lost.
5. On special dates—birthdays, anniversaries of marriage, or even death, and so forth—offer to *celebrate* (i.e., reminisce) with a special dinner out or send flowers or a card.

Nourishment

I have heard, more than once, that when someone dies, you should take food to the grieving family. I suspect it is a more widespread custom than just in the south, which is where I learned it. I can understand the instinct that makes us want to nourish those who are grieving. I think that instinct must tell us that the ones left behind are starving on some level, and food is the only tangible thing we can think of to satisfy that hunger (even though it is likely to be more emotional than physical). We just don't always know what else we can do, and food is a small thing we can offer in the immediate moment to give some measure of comfort. But when the survivor is a single person left behind, how can he or she possibly eat all that food—alone? And does that person really want to sit there all alone trying to force leftover casserole down, when every bite is flavored by tears?

Perhaps the best gift we can give is ourselves, and if nutritious food comes with that gift, so much the better. Rather than deliver a casserole to be eaten in solitude, would it not be better to join your grieving friend for that meal? Invite your friend to your home. Take him or her out to eat. Or, if your friend simply cannot find the motivation to dress and leave home, take the food to your friend's house and stay and eat with them, even if it means your friend is eating in their pajamas because he or she could not find the energy for anything more. You cannot take the place of the person who is gone, but you can be a loving, caring face across the table. You can offer conversation and companionship with each bite. You can toast the person who is absent and make that person an honorary guest at the meal. Maybe the dinner will pass with a little less pain. Maybe you will help nourish more than an empty belly. And maybe, just maybe, you will help nourish an empty heart.

A Soft Place to Fall

When I realize the depth of grief my friends Joy and Betts (and other precious friends and family) live with every day, my heart cries out to help, to mend what hurts. But no amount of compassion will ever let me know the path they walk day after day, year after year. That's the hard part of seeing someone I care so much about suffering. I can see the pain, but I can never fully understand, even if I suffer a similar loss. Each person's grief is unique, and everyone must experience it in his or her own way, in their own time. Some grieve silently. Some loudly and publicly. Some move on quickly. Some never do. No one way is right or wrong. It just is. All I can do is be there with open arms and an open heart to give my grieving friends a soft place to fall when the grief becomes too much to bear, and accept them as they are in that moment.

"Some of the most comforting words in the universe are *me too*. That moment when you find out that your struggle is also someone else's struggle that you're not alone, and that others have been down the same road."
— *Unknown*

The Other Players

Widow. Widower. The very words speak to us of loss, of pain, of heartache that only time can ease. As the solitary spouse or significant other who is left behind, you become the sole focus for those of us who love you. We look for ways to comfort you in whatever way we can. We reach out to you. We offer hugs and food and time and companionship. This is as it should be. You have suffered an overwhelming loss, and your whole world is colored by grief. You are just trying to make it through one moment at a time. The most natural and kindest first thing for us to do is to ask, "How are YOU?"

But what about the others around you who are also left behind? The mothers and fathers, brothers and sisters, and children and best friends? Who comforts them? It is not up to you. You are mourning more deeply than anyone who has not been there can know. I think the other players, as I call them, become the forgotten ones in a world defined by grief. When someone dies, so much focus shifts in a single direction that all the other loved ones simply become secondary. In trying to comfort the wife or husband or significant other, we forget to ask how the next tier of loved ones are doing. And make no mistake, they are grieving too. They need comfort just as they try to offer it.

When my friend Betts's husband transitioned after a valiant fight with cancer, there is no question she was mourning deeply. She still is. But her sister, who had lived with or very near them for over half her life, was grieving almost as deeply as Betts. Jerry was like a father to her, and yet no one ever asked her how she was doing. What a sad, lonely feeling that must have been. And yet, in the face of her own grief, she unselfishly put her life on hold to stay with and comfort her sister. Perhaps they found a measure of solace in comforting one another.

I remember when my mother died mere months before my thirteenth birthday. Young as we were, my younger brother and I knew the implications of what had happened, that we would see our mother no more, and that life as we knew it was irrevocably changed. We understood. We were confused and grieving deeply and yet as children, we were given little thought as others sought ways to comfort our father, our older sister, and themselves. I don't recall ever being asked how I was doing. I mourned my mother alone for decades afterward, always afraid to show the sorrow, keeping it hidden deep within my own heart, and never asking for help in dealing with the grief. I think that the child I was when my grief was ignored came to believe that she was not entitled to grieve because no one offered her comfort. Perhaps never knowing comfort is why I so often do not know how to comfort anyone who is grieving.

I know it can be heartbreaking and exhausting to offer solace in the face of deep grief, especially when you are mourning too, but simply and genuinely asking, "How are YOU doing, how are you REALLY doing?" may well be the greatest and yet simplest gift you can offer, not only to the loved one in black, but also to those next closest ones, the other players, who may well be near invisible in their threads of gray.

Breathing Again

Everybody Needs Somebody

I had called twice. No answer, just voice mail. After the second call, I started to worry. Our friend was barely a week out of the hospital following back surgery. At first, he had stayed with his son, but now he had been home alone for several days. Fortunately, before we could go up to check on him in person, he came hobbling down the stairs to meet us. Everything was fine.

But what if he had not been fine? What if he had fallen and was unable to get up or reach his cell phone? How long would he have lain on the floor hoping, praying for help?

This was a very real situation that made me think of all the people in my life who live alone. Some are widowed. Some are divorced. Some have been alone for a long time and have learned survival skills. Others are new at the loneliness game and so immersed in grief that they do not consider what can happen if no one notices how long it's been since anyone saw or talked to them.

I know this danger becomes greater with age. When you have to show up every day for work, people notice when you are not there. Retirement, on the other hand, can be a whole different circumstance. Throw in an absence of immediate family or close friends on top of losing the anchor that was your soul mate, and who is there to notice when you drop off the grid?

Now I know you may desperately want to isolate yourself in your grief. Many people do. That is normal. But know that one day, that will change. And also know that even as you seek solitude, there are those of us in your life who care about you and want to help in any way we can. That includes simply staying in contact, however briefly.

I used to see the "Help, I've fallen and can't get up" life alert commercials as something of a joke. Now I understand the value of those devices. But if you are grieving and alone, that is so impersonal. One friend of mine has made an arrangement with an acquaintance to send him a daily "good morning" text just to let him know, as she says, she made it to another day. As a widow, that has sometimes been a major accomplishment for her, but even when she most wanted to be alone, it was something she could do without too much interaction. And it was safe.

Know that it is okay to ask for help. In fact, I know I would be honored to be trusted or needed like that by any of my friends. The fact is, everybody needs somebody sometimes. And there is never a better sometime than when you are at your lowest.

Breaching Walls

The ones we love who are immersed in grief, may retreat to something akin to a walled island. Not understanding their mourning, we try to draw them out from behind the solid walls they have built. We want to help, but we do not know how. Although we can build ladders and doors over and through the walls, we cannot enter the inner recesses. They are reserved for the one who mourns. One day, when they are ready, they will reach a hand through the wall. When they do, let them find your loving embrace. Let them see that you are waiting there just a step beyond their wall, that they are not alone.

Cathy Marley

Digging Out

Buried beneath the rubble
Of fallen chances,
I cry for rescue.
But no one comes.

Waiting in the dark,
I pound bloody fists
On unfeeling stone.
Even God seems deaf.

Until I begin to dig.
I move a stone.
And then another
To save myself.

Deep in rubble,
I cannot hear.
I cannot see
Beyond the darkness.

On the other side,
A rescuer digs.
She calls my name.
She shines a light.

Together we dig
Until I hear her voice,
See her light
And will myself to freedom.

No Two Ways to Mourn

The second principle of From Grief to Peace says, *I have the right to mourn the loss of my soul mate in my own way.*[1] As a friend, I can revise that to say, *My loved one has the right to mourn the loss of their soul mate in his or her own way.* My responsibility is to allow my friend to do just that but to provide a loving, nonjudgmental safe haven when he or she can no longer do it alone.

I think one of the most difficult parts of having a friend who is lost in grief is to see the depth of that person's pain and want to fix it. We would like to believe that we know what will help, even if we have never personally experienced such loss. And the impulse to share that knowledge can be huge. The more we care, the more we want to help.

Early in life, we learn from our mothers that when someone has a boo-boo, a kiss and a hug can make it all better. After all, mommy knows best, right? Well, losing a soul mate may well be one of the biggest boo-boos we can ever experience as an adult. It hurts. It really hurts.

And just as a mother must sometimes allow her

children to work through a hurt on their own, so, too, must those of us who want to help a grieving loved one allow that person to mourn in whatever way is right for him or her. I have seen friends whose mourning takes the form of frequent and distant traveling. Perhaps spending time in such unfamiliar surroundings is that person's way of escaping the desperately sad emptiness and reminders of his or her loss. Another dear friend appears to have found solace in moving to a new home and making new friends—lots of them. I suspect it may be her way of dealing with the isolation that developed as she cared for a dying husband. I also suspect she sometimes cries behind her new closed door. I don't think either response would be the right one for me, but I cannot ever allow myself to judge how anyone chooses to mourn.

Grief is intensely personal. No two losses can ever be the same. Each relationship is unique. Each couple is unique. How, then, can we expect anyone to follow some set formula decided upon by society or doctors or peers or anyone other than the one who is living with loss? And yet, in some ways we do. I think those formulas are perhaps just a little bit too easy an answer. They ignore the major variable of individuality.

So, what can I, as a friend, do? Probably not as much as I would like to do. But I can lovingly let my grieving friends know that when they are ready to begin moving forward, I will be there to keep them company as they follow the path they must follow, the one they have defined. They do not have to heal alone and in a vacuum. There is love out here for them. Not the same as what they have lost, but love for sure. I can ask how they are doing and really listen to the answer. And yes, I can serve as a judgment-free wailing wall, while they cry their grief to the heavens and my loving ear.

---

[1] © From Grief to Peace, LLC, 2016, www.FromGriefToPeace.org, reprinted by permission.

Breathing Again

Honoring Lost Loves

As more of those I love transition from this world to the next, I find myself looking for ways to honor them and the impact they had on this world, on my life. I do not want to forget them and the wonderful memories we created together. Birthdays, anniversaries, the day they died all have meaning and give us an opportunity to resurrect those memories.

But it is equally important to help grieving friends honor the special days they celebrated with their lost loves.

Last month was an important remembering month for my friends Betts and Joy. Jerry's birthday was in May and John passed away in May as well. The month could be a very sad one for both of my friends so we have started a new tradition. I want them to feel free to talk all they want about these two fine men and to know someone else thinks of them, too. And so, we planned a dinner and lunch in John's and Jerry's honor.

For Jerry, we went to a favorite restaurant where he and Betts had created memories. For John, Norm and I met Joy for a lovely dinner, something they had loved to do together and something Joy rarely does now. On both occasions, we talked about memories. We reminisced over things large and small. And we toasted those who are gone. I think just being able to talk freely about their soul mates and knowing they will not be forgotten gave my friends a small measure of comfort.

Some people plant trees or dedicate meditation benches in a favorite spot or make large donations in honor of lost loved ones. Those are all fitting memorials. But smaller, year-by-year remembrances can be equally meaningful and can serve to keep memories alive. Dinner at a favorite restaurant. A trip to a special place. Fishing on a lake in honor of the fisherman who is gone. A much-loved play or concert with a favorite performer. All are ways we can keep those precious memories alive.

When my soul sister Anita's birthday comes in August, those of us who loved her are already planning to do something to celebrate her life. Don't know yet what we will do, but I know it will be something she would have enjoyed. And next year on the anniversary of her passing and on her birthday, I know we will honor her again, as we will from now on. She had a huge impact on my life. I miss her. And I will do all I can to keep her fresh and alive in our hearts and minds. What better tribute could we offer our loved one's memory?

Breathing Again

Where Did Everyone Go?

In those first days after a soul mate transitions, it sometimes feels like the entire world has descended on you at once. Your home becomes a beehive of activity, noisy and crowded with people wanting to "help." Family flies in from out of town. Neighbors and friends drop by laden with food and condolences. Church members you do not even know gather round. Flowers arrive daily, sometimes even hourly. It feels as though the phone rings constantly. And the mail is flooded with cards expressing sympathy.

Until the funeral.

Afterward, what had been akin to a flooding river soon dwindles away to a mere trickle. One day, you look up and realize you are alone, and the lonely silence is deafening. The food is gone—either eaten or tossed. Flowers have wilted and found their way to the trash. The doorbell has stopped ringing, and the phone has fallen silent except for clueless telemarketers and politicians. And your mail once again contains little more than junk mail and bills. It seems as though they are invariably addressed to your absent loved one, a painful reminder of what you have lost.

Cathy Marley

You wake up one morning to your silent home and ask, "Where did everyone go?"

Indeed. For those who are not grieving, life returns to *normal* ever so quickly. For those who *are* grieving, it feels as though it never will. In that difference lies the failure of those who really do want to help. Somehow, life intrudes and in the absence of the pain of constant sorrow, those of us who are not as close to the grief move on. That does not mean we do not care. It simply means the demands of life have clamored more loudly for our attention than your grief, the grief of someone we love. We fool ourselves into thinking you are *fine* now that the immediate loss is over. In fact, you are far from fine, and the days, weeks, months, even years after the loss are when you need us the most.

So, what can we do to not be one of the missing friends, to help you survive your grief? How can you tell us what you need? The key is for us to not forget about you as you desperately try to move forward alone. At a minimum, we can:
- Calculated as it may sound, make you a permanent part of our to-do list, a priority, if you will.
- Identify the least demanding day and time in our week, and make it a point to use that time to reach out. Call, e-mail, text, anything that will let you know we are still thinking of you.
- Add your important dates—birthdays, anniversaries of marriage and death—to our calendar and, with a lunch or dinner date,

flowers, a card, or anything to remind you that your important dates are still important, let you know we have not forgotten .
- Call and offer to bring a video and pizza for a quiet afternoon or evening of companionship.
- Invite you to join us for shopping, a special event or simply a meal out. We should not be hurt if you are not up to it. Rather, we should be persistent. Eventually, you will say yes.
- And most importantly, no matter what we do with you, we should always strive to help keep your memories alive. This means speaking your loved one's name while recalling special memories and happy times.

Chapter 4
Life Changes

Photo by Cathy Marley

It Takes Patience – Grief Has No Timeline

How are your friends and family handling your grief? If they are pushing you to cut short the time you need to heal, perhaps these thoughts will help them better understand how to relate to you.

I cannot speak for the rest of the world, but I know that having patience is sometimes very difficult for me. I want things fixed right now, not next week or next month or next year—NOW. I think perhaps that is, in part, because I don't like having to deal with sad things or challenges that take much time to resolve. I would much rather live the part of little Mary Sunshine who always sees only the good stuff and chooses to ignore the things that hurt. But life is not like that. Sometimes, the only way to deal with the hard stuff is to just let it happen, to be patient while healing finds a way to settle into the damaged areas.

Today, I feel that way about a dear friend who lies, barely conscious, in ICU after having a burst aneurysm in her brain repaired. Despite all the odds, she is alive and doing amazingly well. For that, I will be eternally grateful. Now all I want is to see her full of life, laughing and loving as she always has. I know that she has a long road to recovery ahead of her, but I want her back right now. All I can do is exercise that ever-elusive patience and stand by her side as she follows the road back to us.

I think there is a lesson for me here. Is the patience I need for my ill friend any different than what I need for those I love who are grieving? I think not. They have suffered a terrible loss, one I can only imagine. Just as my friend's brain is injured and healing, so, too, are my grieving friends' hearts injured and healing. As any physician will tell you, healing takes time, and the time it takes is unique to each and every person. Why then, can anyone expect mourning to follow any set timeline? I sometimes wonder how doctors can know this about physical injuries but not understand that it applies to emotional and psychic pain as well. Grief, like illness or injury, heals on its own schedule, never one that we impose upon it. It will eventually find a way. But, it takes patience for us to allow time to do its job.

Breathing Again

What Gifts Do You Give a Soul Mate Who Is Gone?

This time last year, I was eagerly anticipating my soul sister Anita's annual arrival for Christmas. Every year, she came to Arizona before the holidays and stayed at least until New Year's. Somehow, she always managed to spend some time with all the friends and family she had here in the Valley. Usually, her Christmas visits were the only time in the year when we could hug and talk for hours. The rest of the year, we had to make do with long telephone calls.

But last year was the last time we had for a Christmas together. With no warning, Anita fell ill and transitioned just a week before she was to return home to Oregon. She will not be with us this Christmas, and I am already feeling her absence. It feels as though there is not quite as much to anticipate this year. The Christmas spirit is silent, and I find myself going through the motions of creating the holiday for my family and other friends.

Every now and then when I am shopping, I will see something I know she would have loved. Forgetting for just a moment that she is gone, I will pick it up and start to put it in my shopping basket. And then I remember. I have no one to give that particular gift to.

So, I wonder what gifts I can give to her now. Gifts for her spirit and the generous woman she was, gifts she will see from where she is. Last year, she and our other soul sister Elaine and I shared the gift of time together. I am incredibly grateful that we chose that over material gifts that none of us really needed. The trip we took together in January meant more to all of us than anything money could have bought.

This year, I have decided to give Anita gifts you cannot touch, but gifts anyway.

On the advice of the lovely and sensitive medium, Susanne Wilson, I am starting to meditate and open my heart and mind to Anita's presence. It opens the connection with her spirit. An open heart is a gift that transcends life and death.

I am also talking out loud to her when we are riding in my car. Susanne says her spirit likes my car and is often there with me when I am driving alone. So, I will give her the gift of conversation.

And Elaine and I will include Anita when we are together for our Christmas. It was always an AnitaandElaineandCathy event and this year Elaine and I are determined to keep it that way. I don't know yet exactly how we will do it, but somehow, we will have her spirit with us this first year without her. Keeping her memory alive and with us is a gift of connection.

Breathing Again

Finally, I know there were causes she passionately supported. This Christmas, there will be donations to them in her honor. It is a gift that we can give in her stead.

There will not be a moment of the next month that I do not feel the presence of my dear friend and soul sister.

I know that after losing a soul mate, celebrating a holiday like Christmas is the last thing you want to do. It's hard to feel festive when the one person you want to be there is gone. Shopping for material gifts is pointless. But perhaps there can be a small measure of comfort in connecting with your soul mate's spirit, in keeping the memory alive, in honoring him or her by doing things you would have done together. Celebrating may not feel right, but celebrating what you had together could never be wrong. So, I pose the following question to you. How will you celebrate the soul mate you have lost?

Breathing Again

A New Normal

"Occasionally, weep deeply over the life you hoped would be. Grieve the losses. Then wash your face. Trust God. And embrace the life you have."

– John Piper

This quote came to me via Facebook and it made me think about how it applies to my life.

When I married Norm, I had fallen in love with a good man who was not only handsome, but also intelligent, witty, strong, and virile. I was twenty-seven. He was forty. At the time, the thirteen-year age difference seemed immaterial. We set about living the rest of our life together—active, busy, rewarding on every level. We created a life that lived up to all our expectations and then some. Together, we worked toward common goals, and we traveled and we played. We could not imagine anything different; that is, until the year he turned seventy-two and was diagnosed with a form of lymphoma.

Doctor visits, medications, and hospital stays dominated the eighteen months between onset of his symptoms and the day he finally received that diagnosis. The next six and a half years revolved around month-long treatments every six months. In some ways, not knowing what was wrong was worse than finally having an answer. We thought life would soon just return to the way it had always been.

The good news, the doctor told us, was that the form of lymphoma he had would not kill him. The bad news was that treatment might be needed for the rest of his life. We were told that the side effects would be minimal, primarily allergic reactions. No one mentioned the other potential effects of regularly pumping poison into him for six and a half years.

By the time Norm had stabilized enough to stop treatment, he was nearing his seventy-ninth birthday. Finally, I thought, our life could return to normal, and we could go back to living as we had before the specter of treatments loomed over us. That was four years ago, and life has not returned to *normal*. I don't think it ever will.

At some point, I realized that the man I loved had changed. He had slowed down, way down, both physically and mentally. A gifted engineer, he often had trouble now solving what had previously been simple problems for him. His thought processes had slowed, and somewhere along the way, this once active, vibrant man had started spending hours sitting in front of the television watching reruns of favorite programs. I worried about him. And, much as I hate to admit it, sometimes I grew angry that he seemed to have given up, that he was choosing "stupidity" over the brilliance I knew he was capable of.

Breathing Again

A part of me was angry about all we had lost. And for the longest time, I blamed him. But then I began to see how much worse it could be. One new friend's husband had been battling Parkinson's disease for nineteen years. Their life had steadily gone downhill as he deteriorated and eventually died. Another friend spent months beside her soul mate as lung cancer took his life—and much of hers. And yet another friend's husband died suddenly, leaving her alone and grieving deeply. Each of them had lost something profound and precious, someone who was the center of their world, but I never saw them angry about it. Oh, they grieved. Oh, my God, how they grieved. And I am sure they had their moments of anger behind closed doors. But they also accepted that they couldn't change anything about what had happened.

I began to look at the changes in our lifestyle and in Norm with new eyes. I realized that what he was going through had nothing to do with choice. These changes were little more than side effects of life-saving treatments that had a greater impact on him and on us than I had realized. Perhaps those changes were inevitable with age, but the treatments made them become more obvious to me in a short time. It felt like he had gone from young to old overnight and I was not prepared for that. My perspective changed with one simple insight. He could have DIED but he was still ALIVE, and I still had this incredible man in my life. So what if he was a little diminished from the man I had known and loved for so long? This is what "in sickness and in health" is all about. We just don't think about it when, as starry-eyed newlyweds, we say the words.

Cathy Marley

I began to look for ways to treasure what I now realize must be normal from now on. I just accepted that I need to rely less on him and more on me and be grateful I am able to do that. I watch for the glimmers of my old Norm. And I find them: a spark of humor here, a little teasing there, the conversations that slip briefly to the old depths. Our world is a little smaller now. Gone are the big exciting trips and cruises. Rather, we now find our enjoyment in dinner dates, the occasional afternoon movie or an evening out for a jazz concert and dinner.

It is a new way of living for us, one based on the knowledge that none of us stays young forever, none of us stays the same for a lifetime, and none of us lives forever. While I am so very fortunate to still have Norm with me, what the last few years have brought is a death of sorts, a death of the life we once so deeply enjoyed together. So yes, I mourn the changes in my soul mate and I have grieved for what we have lost, but I trust that life has turned out as it should have. This life is our new normal, and I embrace it with all my heart.

You Can Do It ... Taking on New Roles

In every relationship, each individual has a whole spectrum of roles they play. He's the handyman. She's the chef. Maybe she pays the bills, and he does all the shopping. In the case of illness, the roles are very predictable. The illness dictates care receiver and caregiver. But in other relationships, where there is no illness, we just tend to fall into our roles as time goes by. It is part of a healthy relationship that we assume the roles most suited to our individual talents and skills. But what do you do when half of your team is suddenly gone? You adapt. And you learn you can do far more than you ever thought you could.

When I first married Norm, we were both working full-time with an hour commute each way. And, we operated an 80-acre alfalfa farm to boot. Add in that Norm frequently traveled for work and you get an idea that we had to operate as a highly functioning team just to get everything done. It didn't take long for the physical work and vehicle maintenance to fall on his shoulders, while the house, books, bills, and taxes fell on mine. It was an arrangement that worked for the whole family.

In time, we sold the farm and when we were

ready, we both retired, pretty much. Over the years, we found our roles changing as time and age caught up to us. Eventually we even gave ourselves permission to hire people to do some of the things that became a challenge for us. A landscaping crew. A housekeeper to clean every two weeks. A pool man. A service department to keep the cars running. You get the idea.

We learned that we could not do everything. But right now, I do still have Norm in my life to help with some of the things that we must still do on our own, things like emptying the trash, feeding the pets, the laundry, and making the coffee in the morning. He makes good coffee.

Over the years, we have each had our roles, but now the roles are reversing, changing, growing. As age has sapped strength in us both and naturally forced us to slow down, I have found myself picking up the slack in things I have never had to do before. It's part of the natural ebb and flow of a relationship.

I don't know what I would do without him here. I sometimes wonder how I would manage to get everything done. And then I realize that somehow, I have always managed to do what needs to be done. We all do.

I think of my friends who have lost their soul mate and are now completely alone in an empty house or who have also become the primary caregiver for an aging parent. I have read stories of widowed fathers who quickly learn to braid hair and give makeup advice to young daughters. They all pretty much must do everything on their own. And they manage. As can you. Despite the grief of losing the one person in the world you loved beyond reason, you will manage. You will learn to do stuff you never thought you could. You may be upset, angry, and not want to do the new things. But you must do them. You can do them. You will find people who can do things for you. A handyman. An electrician. A talented hairdresser. A yard crew. A team to handle the things you know nothing about. Like the fathers learning how to mother daughters, you may even add new tools to your personal toolbox. Each new role you take on is another reminder of what you have lost. It is a constant reminder. But as you do handle each new challenge, you will hear a voice in your head from the other side telling you, "I knew you could do it!"

Breathing Again

I've Got a Guy for That

Not too long ago, I was talking with two friends, both of them alone after having lived with husbands who were always equal partners in the effort it takes to maintain a household. For years those two men could be relied on to make sure everything ran smoothly. But then one day they were gone, leaving my friends to figure out ways to maintain their car, fix the plumbing, repair broken appliances and houses, and so on.

I quickly realized that every time one of us encounters a new problem—Joy's scorpions in the house, Betts's irrigation leaks, and my inoperative landscape lighting, for example—one or the other of us will invariably step in, saying, "Oh, I've got a guy for that." So now, we have teams in place that we share. Joy and I use the same yard guys. Betts uses my irrigation and garage repair guys. And we are all sharing resources as we move toward the ultimate publication of our books.

Once upon a time I, much like Joy and Betts, always relied on my Norm to handle things like car repairs, yard maintenance, the pool, and any problem that could be solved by his excellent engineering mind. But as the years have passed, I find that more and more, he is reluctant to take on those tasks. I think part of it is a result of over six years of treatment for lymphoma. The treatments affected him more deeply than we realized at the time, but I can still bounce problems off him and ask for his advice. I can only imagine how difficult it would be to have him gone completely.

So, over time, I have built my team of "guys for that." The yard guys keep the weeds from taking over the world. Thanks to my pool guy, the pool is always sparkling. I have a team that maintains our two fountains monthly. There is the contractor who can always be relied upon to either fix things or recommend someone who can. The electrician, the air conditioning people, the plumbers, the garage door guy, the accountant, the financial advisor, and the doctors. The list goes on forever, but the fact is that things eventually get done, not neglected.

I never realized how much we can no longer do as we age or as we find ourselves alone, but there it is. That's why I have those teams of guys. They keep my day-to-day world humming and my surroundings livable. All of them came to me via word of mouth recommendations.

But then there is the other team of "guys." They are the ones you call when the pain just becomes more than you can handle, or when you are sick and need someone who loves you to hold your hand and spoon chicken soup into your mouth, or when something goes bump in the night and you need someone to vanquish the closet monsters. Those are the "guys" who love you unconditionally and will be there for you for however long you need them. They are the ones who will take up a sword and fight alongside you, defending your fragile self as you make your way through this perilous minefield called grief. They are the ones who will come if only you can find the strength to call. They are the ones who will hear "I need you" and fly to your side. They are the sincerest form of "guys for that." I call them friends and family. Some call them angels.

No More Days

As I prepared a Celebration of Life for my beloved soul sister Anita, I thought of all the moments we took for granted, especially those in the days we did not realize would be her last. She had been living far away from those of us who loved her for many years, but she always tried to be with us for Christmas. That last year, Anita came to Arizona for a brief time in October to celebrate our birthdays—my seventieth and the kickoff to Elaine's sixtieth as well as her own seventieth.

The highlight of that trip was an evening out at Circus Vargas, Elaine, Anita and me, something we planned together. Like a trio of children with dancing eyes, we laughed and thrilled to the joy of the circus. Acrobats, clowns, lights, music, glitz, and magic! And it *was* a magical evening, one to be remembered always. But we were casual about the memories, confident there would be many more such times and so thought nothing of postponing other outings until we could come together again at Christmas.

We waited because we knew there would be more days to do all the things we loved. There were always more days.

And sure enough, Christmas did roll around. Sooner than we, in all our busyness, expected. But Christmas is such a full season and we knew we had plenty of time. Anita came and spent her first two weeks with family as it should be. The next two she spent with Elaine, something that had been put off for years until Elaine finally had her own home again. Again, as it should be.

Once the holidays were behind us, we piled in the car together and made a trip south to the resort town of Tubac, just three dear girlfriends on an exciting day trip to shop, laugh, and love one another. We were creating more memories that day. Margaritas and Mexican food under an umbrella. Shopping like we would never see Mexican pottery again. And talking, talking, talking for hours. How were we to know it would be our last trip, our last chance to create such precious memories?

Looking forward to shopping and dinners and movies together, Anita and I saved our time for the end of her visit. After all, there would be plenty of days to do all the things we loved. There were always more days. But this time there were no more.

Instead, there was a hospital. Surgery. Medical ups and downs. And then more downs than ups. And finally, hospice. The weeks we had planned to play were spent in the very serious business of saying a final goodbye and dying. Suddenly, there were no more days. Things left undone would never come to be. We would create no more happy memories. Time ran out and she was gone.

Whenever I see a news report of some tragedy involving many deaths, I keep coming back to the fact that each of the people who died, victim and perpetrator alike, was loved by someone at some point in their life. Some of them were probably also soul mates to someone who will now be left mourning that horrible, senseless loss. In an instant, that love on this plane was snuffed out. The love will not die with death, but what remains will be a much lonelier form of love.

For those of us who remain behind after a death, one major lesson to learn is that although today may be the first day of the rest of your life, it could just as easily be the last of yours or of someone you love. Reminding ourselves to cherish every moment, to forgive more, to play more, and to tell those we love how much we respect and admire them helps us keep our relationships clean before we are thrown into that final separation.

Perhaps our purpose in life is to live the days we are given as fully and joyfully as we can so that when we are gone, people will remember us as someone who embodied love and enriched their lives. I am sure that looks a little different for each of us and is not always easy, especially when we are consumed by grief. But in our hearts, we know when we are living to that purpose and when we are not. The times we are not are the times we begin to "should" on ourselves or demand impossible levels of perfection from ourselves and others.

Cathy Marley

In losing my soul sister, Anita, I learned to make time now for creating memories with those I love, something far more important than cleaning a house or paying bills or dealing with any one of the many things I have always thought were so important. In reality, none of them matter. We can plan to create time somewhere in the future with those we love, but there are no guarantees. Tomorrow may not come. Fate does not see our busy calendar. It only knows now. And so today I will love as if there is no tomorrow. Today, I will store every sight and sound and taste and sensation in the vault of memory for the time that eventually comes for us all—when there are no more days.

Chapter 5
Signs/Soul Mate Connections

Photo by Cathy Marley

Look for the Quick Hellos

I believe our loved ones send us signs from the other side. In my case, I am convinced that I get feathers and pennies from my soul sister Anita, from my parents, and from my guardians. How do I know they are signs? They are the ones that appear in places they don't belong, or come when I am thinking of that person, or when I need a little extra support. Those, I believe, are signs. The feather I found under a chair in the Barnes and Noble café after one of our From Grief to Peace Meetings? Definitely a sign that Anita was there and approved. The feathers that show up below a bird's nest or amid other indications of a cat's guilty feast? Probably not.

There is a fine line between reality and delusion. Some people, in their grief, can become a little too carried away with the spiritual manifestations of their lost one. An odd noise becomes a spirit. A spirit becomes a ghost. And suddenly you are haunted.

My friend Joy gets signs from her John all the time, and they are very clearly signs, sometimes very powerful ones. She talks about many of them in her book, *I Will Never Leave You*. But what we think are signs may not always be signs. When John was still alive, they lived in a house they were pretty sure was haunted. One night, Joy kept hearing a rhythmical noise somewhere around her dresser. The spirit, she was sure, was trying to communicate with them—until she realized the noise was only her beeper going off and vibrating on the wooden dresser. Spirits are rarely that rhythmical. Sometimes the noise is just a beeper. Sometimes it really is a sign. Listen for the beeper but be open to the times it is more.

This last week at a wedding reception, I started talking with an acquaintance whose husband died almost a year ago. As we talked about him, she told me she often catches glimpses of him out of the corner of her eye but when she looks, nothing is there. How does she know it is him? She can *feel* his presence every time. Betts has had similar experiences with her Jerry, seeing him just on the edge of vision in Las Vegas, one of their favorite places, having a hibiscus flower twirl, untouched, five times in a bowl of water as she thought of him, having the lid fly off a trash can when Jerry came up in conversation. Those are signs.

So how do *you* know it is a sign and not delusion or wishful thinking? It may reflect a special song or date or animal that means something just to you or the two of you. Or, it may feel like a little internal hug. Or a gentle tickle in the brain that says, *Hey, look at this.* Somehow, you really feel that person at that moment, like a quick hello. And it is those quick hellos that keep you going.

Breathing Again

Photo by Cathy Marley

Grieving Beau

In late September, I started finding feathers—one every day for the first few days and then not quite that often, but still they came to me when I least expected to see them. At first, they were real feathers from common birds, nothing especially unusual, just feathers. And then a more permanent form, including a lovely sculpted pewter feather that spoke to my heart and begged to be mine. The day the first feather appeared planted upright in gravel, I was leaving a Life in the Afterlife conference and had been talking with my friends Betts and Joy about signs we receive from the other side. Feathers are a very common sign, so I knew at some level that the feathers were a message. I just did not know who was sending them or why.

I do now.

You see, the first feather I noticed came to me shortly after our precious cat Beau's first "birthday" as a member of our family. I picked it up and saved it, putting it near my computer monitor where I could reflect on its meaning every day. Well, Beau, being the great hunter he was in his mind, decided that feather and the two that followed must be a bird in some form and so he tried to eat them all. I salvaged those wet, bedraggled feathers and put them away in my desk drawer. Subsequent feathers were saved from his natural predatory instincts in like manner. I really did not give it a second thought, and in time the appearance of fresh feathers dwindled.

In early November, Joy, Betts, and I celebrated my birthday with a lovely lunch outside on the patio at T. Cooks, an elegant restaurant in central Phoenix. Toward the end of our meal as we talked animatedly, Betts was waving a French fry in the air as she finished a comment when suddenly, a good-sized bird swooped across the table and snatched that fry right out of her hand. Amazed at its bravado, I attached no particular significance to the mock attack.

Breathing Again

I do now.

And then, the unthinkable happened. Sweet, innocent Beau decided somewhere in his kitty brain that it would be a good idea to go on a real adventure. In a moment of distraction on my part, he slipped outside and was gone without my even realizing it. I spent a fruitless day searching every corner of our house for him, hoping he was just hiding. But he was gone. We posted flyers. I registered his photo with every rescue website that would allow it. His microchip company notified all the vets and rescue groups in the area. We sent an e-mail blast to every house in the neighborhood. I visited the pound, shelters, and the Humane Society and posted his face there. Always the message was the same, "This beautiful cat is lost and he is loved. If you see him, please, please help him come home."

In a final act of desperation, I contacted a gifted pet intuitive, Debbie Johnstone, who felt very strongly that our Beau was still in this world and hiding. The sense was that he was more interested in the experience and adventure he was having than he was frightened. We searched and we called, and we sent him messages on how to find his way home. Nothing worked. I think now that perhaps it was never meant to. Two days after we reached him psychically, a neighbor from a block away called. He had found a very small paw and remnants of fur from what appeared to be a white cat. I was so sure our Beau was safe that I could not believe it could be him. Still, I contacted Debbie to reassure me that he was still alive. But that was not meant to be.

All the signs Debbie saw told her he had

transitioned from this life to the next. And, finally, the significance of the feathers came to me. You see, Beau told Debbie he saw a huge bird just before he left this plane. I believe he was taken from us by a great horned owl that had haunted our neighborhood in recent months. We had heard him and seen him, and now he had taken my Beau from me. I think the feathers may have been sent to me to prepare me for what was coming and for how Beau would leave us. The very day he died, I saw yet another feathery reminder in a magazine—lovely white feather-shaped Christmas ornaments with their tips dipped in gold (and yes, I did find and buy them). What a perfect reminder of this pure white boy who, with his young, playful spirit, brought us such joy in his short life. Yes, the feathers may signify the owl that took his life, but remember angels have feathery wings too. Perhaps the feathers I found were from angels trying to send me a measure of peace in advance of my grief.

I think it is important for me to remember that "our" place was my office where I write and where I struggled to find direction in the writing I was doing for From Grief to Peace. Beau was very much a part of what I do here, and I felt his presence here as I wrote this about him. I think perhaps he came into my life and left it far too soon in part to help me understand the grief my friends knew after losing their soul mates. I cannot compare the grief I felt on losing Beau to theirs. Each of us must experience grief in our own way. And I know some losses are greater than others. That does not make the grief I felt on losing Beau any more or less. It was just different. And it was mine. I found myself wrapped in feelings of guilt (could I have done anything differently to change the outcome?), utter sadness (oh God, I hope he did not suffer!) and anger (I briefly wished I could kill that owl), but most of all, there was the pain of knowing I would never again cuddle a warm, purring Beau or laugh at his silly antics.

I know my friends have gone through similar but surely more intense feelings, and this loss helped me understand their pain, their continued mourning. Losing my Beau finally helped me clarify what I am doing with From Grief to Peace. I now see my role so much more clearly. I have never lost a soul mate. But in knowing this loss, I believe I can become a voice for those close friends and family who desperately want to relate to and help a loved one who has lost a soul mate—to help them find their way to peace.

When Beau first came to us, he was the tiniest of kittens, small enough to fit in one hand. And he was the purest, most trusting soul. His pure white color made me want to name him after an angel, but Norm convinced me otherwise. And Beau he became. He taught me to love more deeply, to allow myself to be vulnerable, and to know that there is more than just this one life on this plane of existence. Those feathers and the message they sent over the months confirmed that. The slightly bedraggled (as though Beau had been at it) one that appeared the morning I wrote this did too. I feel strongly that my Beau sent it to me to tell me that he is in a place where he will always be happy and young at heart. Perhaps he was always meant to be an angel after all.

Breathing Again

Signs or Coincidence?

I have learned to watch for signs for what they are—communication from my loved ones and guides in the spirit world. I believe they reach out to us in ways they think we will see, and I am sure each of us is receptive to different signs in their many forms.

For me, signs often take the form of feathers. As I mentioned, it started with my sweet cat Beau. For two months before his transition, my spirit guides began sending me feathers. Just one at a time and often in the unlikeliest of places to catch my attention. Once I got the message after Beau was gone that he is well and happy where he is, the number dwindled.

To this day, I still find feathers when anything important, stressful, or traumatic is happening in my life. I think the spirits realize I am especially attuned to seeing them, so that is what they send me most often. Illness such as having two of my adult children diagnosed with cancer? Feathers. Death such as when my son and my soul sister Anita transitioned? Feathers. The number picks up noticeably before and after anything serious happens, so I have learned to notice them and then steel myself to watch for something to happen. I know they are signs of support. They tell me my loved ones in the spirit world have my back.

But then there are also dreams. In the night before she left us, Anita came to me in a very vivid dream to say goodbye and let me know that she was going someplace she wanted to be. I know it was a visit not just a dream because it is still vivid in my mind more than a year later. The dream visit as she left this plane of existence gave me great peace when she was gone. I think she knew I would need the strength it gave me in the following weeks.

And of course, for me there were elephants. For years, Anita collected them with their trunks raised for good fortune. Most were gifts from me. I could never resist buying one if it was unique, but before she died, I had not seen more than one or two in quite some time. And believe me, I was always on the lookout for them. The week after Anita passed, I found herds of them in a local home décor store. Everywhere I looked, I saw elephants, all with their trunks raised to the heavens. What a mass of good fortune they were! Seeing them before me as I walked through the door of the store was like a huge hello from Anita. Again, I believe it was her way of telling me that she was still with me and had finally found the good fortune she sought for so long.

And the day before we celebrated her life, I heard from her again in the form of two bright pennies lying on the ground. I think it was her way of sending her approval of our plans. Yet another quick hello.

Now I know some will call this all a coincidence,

Breathing Again

that I was attuned to seeing what I wanted to see. But I still keep finding feathers where they do not belong. And I still see far more elephants than is normal.

On the day our son Dale died, we entered hospice for the first time. Directly in front of the doors was a fireplace, and sitting on the hearth was a tall elephant figurine with its trunk raised high. An elephant! Really? I think it was Anita's way of telling me that she would be there to welcome our Dale on the other side.

So, I choose to believe feathers and elephants are messages. And who will prove me wrong?

Our mutual friend, Elaine, is one of the skeptics. I respect her position. She is, after all, a doctor and so expects scientific proof for much that I believe on faith. But I see the signs Anita has sent her even as she fails to recognize them. A "coincidental" visit to the Arizona Science Museum where she just happened to take the time to watch a video about the same brain aneurysm that took our Anita from us. And it was recorded by the surgeon who had performed one of Anita's surgeries. Coincidence? Maybe. But I think it could have been a sign sent in a form that she, as a doctor, would most easily relate to. In preparing for the Celebration of Life, she went shopping for something new and special to wear. What did she find? A lovely top in especially flattering colors for her, although colors she does not normally wear. And on the front, a fascinating jungle image featuring a prominent elephant with its trunk raised triumphantly to the heavens. Coincidence? Wellllll, maybe. But then again, maybe not.

Cathy Marley

I think Anita sent us both signs in the weeks after she passed. They came in ways we would see through our individual filters and maybe, just maybe accept. Mine came in the form of material surprises she knows I will recognize. Elaine's were a bit more overt and targeted her need for very clear statements. All I know for sure is that since she died, she has been speaking to me, and the message I have been getting is that she is still with us—just in a slightly different place. I can no longer pick up the telephone and call her as I could the last years when she was in Oregon and I was in Arizona. But I think she is still very much present in my life. I just need to look and to listen more closely. The signs are there.

At Anita's Celebration of Life, Elaine read a poem entitled *Do Not Stand at My Grave and Weep* by Mary Elizabeth Frye. It is often read at funerals and Celebrations of Life, but I believe Anita sent it to us this time. We found it among her things as we were searching for photos to create a DVD and anything we could include for the event. That she would have saved it is not particularly surprising. That was very much Anita. What was surprising, was that at the bottom, she had written

>Dear Family & Friends,
>Yes, I am here . . . I am always here.
>Anita

Coincidence? Maybe. But then again, maybe not.

Breathing Again

Do Not Stand at My Grave and Weep

"Do not stand at my grave and weep.
I am not there; I do not sleep.

I am a thousand winds that blow.
I am the diamond glints on snow.
I am the sunlight on ripened grain.
I am the gentle autumn rain.

When you awaken in the morning's hush
I am the swift uplifting rush
Of quiet birds in circled flight.
I am the soft stars that shine at night.

Do not stand at my grave and cry;
I am not there; I did not die".

– Mary Elizabeth Frye, 1932

Breathing Again

Photo by Cathy Marley

The Grandma Book and Messages from Beyond

I think sometimes we don't realize how much someone means to us until they are gone. Conversely, I think we also don't realize how much we meant to them until they can no longer reach out to us on this plane. That part is a little more difficult to get.

That was the case with our friend, Shirley.

Shirley was a writer friend we knew from our days in Women Writers of the Desert. When the group folded, there were six of us who were determined to stay in touch with one another: Joy, Betts, Virginia, Vivian, Shirley, and me. Every month or two, we would meet for lunch at the Cheesecake Factory and just catch up on one another's lives over tea and unhealthy portions of good food followed by decadent cheesecake.

Always, Shirley would bring out her Grandma Book, photos of her children and precious grandchildren. The photos never changed. Neither did the pride with which she showed them to each of us in turn. In time, that tattered book became something of a joke, but we went along with it because it meant so much to Shirley to share it. None of us realized how much that friendship and acceptance meant to her.

Shirley transitioned to the next level on September 11, 2016. It caught us all by surprise. We had not seen one another is several months. You know how it is. Despite our best intentions, life takes over.

But since Shirley transitioned, she has communicated from the other side with Joy, Betts, and me in one way or another. The first time she made her presence known was shortly after she left us. She came forward in a reading Betts had with Susanne Wilson, the lovely Carefree Medium, and asked that we be sure to have lunch at the Cheesecake Factory one more time, eating cheesecake and toasting her with tea. And so, we did. We just missed the Grandma Book and Shirley.

Breathing Again

Two weeks later, Shirley called me on my cell phone. When I saw the Face Time message with her name and photo on it appear in my recent calls list, it seemed strange, but I thought it must be one of her kids calling me, going through her contacts list to notify friends of her death. Of course it couldn't be Shirley! I called back, but got no answer and didn't leave a message.

Now the strange part. The next day, I got another call from the same number, which I answered. The man demanded to know who I was and why I was calling. I explained but he insisted he had no idea who Shirley was and that he had not called me. Now, he may have Shirley's old telephone number but I'm pretty sure my number would no longer be in the contact list when that number was reassigned. All I can figure is that Shirley called somehow to thank us for the lunch.

Since then, Shirley always seems to show up when Susanne sees my people during a reading such as the group reading we attended. Sure enough, Shirley dropped in to say hi. As Susanne described her, she said the woman she saw was talking about cheesecake. "Shirley!" we all declared at once.

The more I think about it, the more I realize our infrequent lunches must have been something of a lifeline for Shirley whose home life seemed to be less than ideal. Perhaps we meant more to her than any of us realized while she was still alive. Now, she comes to us via readings and a telephone call that could only have

Cathy Marley

come from beyond to let us know how much our friendship meant to her, to say thank you, if you will. This afterlife connection with her has taught me that no act of kindness goes unappreciated. Even the ones that mean showing interest in a Grandma Book you have seen many times before. Thanks to Shirley, I think I have become more deeply committed to showing kindness throughout my life. Isn't it wonderful to know that those small acts can carry over beyond this life?

Breathing Again

How Do We Recognize Our Soul Mate?

What is it that lets us know our soul mate when we meet in this lifetime? There is, for sure, a soul knowing that comes, but I think there must be other, more tangible things we recognize. A smile. A certain sparkle in the eyes. The electric energy of a familiar aura. I just know the attraction is there and inevitable.

And I believe, too, that each of us is, in our truest essence, a being of light. Perhaps it is that light we recognize across lifetimes.

Light

Oh, your light.
It glowed
With such a lovely warmth.

I felt its caress
In your eyes.
I kissed it
In your smile.
I touched it
In your soul.

Cathy Marley

Oh, your light.
It knew me
From lifetimes ago.

I knew it
Here.
I loved it
Before.
I will cherish it
Always.

Oh, your light
Calls to mine
Across time and space.

Rejoined,
Two lights become one.
A sparkling swirl,
Our light celebrates.
An eternal flame
Is born.

Chapter 6
Healing and Finding Peace

Photo by Cathy Marley

Little Things

I think we go through life all too often taking those we love for granted. That's really just how life is. We treasure the relationship. No question about that. Sometimes we may argue, but we always love. Perhaps we show it in small gestures. A smile. A "remember when?" memory. A laugh shared over some silly joke just between the two of you. Or just a reach across the bed in the darkness of night. Small things for sure, but a critical part of the warp and woof of your life together.

We may not see that person we love so much every day or we may wake to their face and fall asleep at their side. They may live miles and miles away from us or in the same house. But somehow we always know they are there across the room, at the end of a telephone line, an e-mail, a Facebook post, or even the other end of a road.

Their presence is a part of the air we breathe. And like breathing, we may simply stop thinking of them consciously—until one day they are gone, and we cannot reach them in any of our usual ways. It is then that we think back to those small moments, the little

Cathy Marley

things that brought a smile to our heart, that gave substance to a love that could not be defined. Those are the moments that will lift us up and help us move through our grief to a measure of peace.

Breathing Again

The Call that Never Comes

The month before she left us forever, my dear soul sister Anita saw a lively variety show, *The Rhythm Cats*, in far east Mesa, Arizona, with her family and could not praise the show highly enough. I don't think I had ever seen her so excited about a live performance. She insisted that we three sisters of the heart—she, Elaine and I—simply had to go together, but I was in no rush to go as it represented a pretty long drive. Well, as fate would have it, less than a month later she was in the hospital, and we lost her before we could share that experience. Somehow the length of the drive felt trivial after that, and I regretted not feeling more urgency to see the show with her.

But Elaine had kept the flyer Anita gave us afterward, and for my birthday she made reservations for us to see the show together. Anita was not there physically, but I am sure her spirit was there with us and dancing in the aisles to a blend of music that ranged from Willie Nelson and Dion and the Belmonts to big band and Rimsky-Korsakov. In her absence, it was a bittersweet evening, but still more of a tribute to her and the experiences we would never again have together than it was a birthday celebration. It was just what we needed.

Cathy Marley

Always before, I knew that on the day of my birthday, Anita would call. She would send cards and gifts too, but always she would call. That meant more than any material gift ever could. Just hearing her voice reaching out across the miles to me in love was enough. The first year after her death, I had lots of sweet birthday wishes in the form of calls, gifts, cards, Facebook messages, and special meals. I deeply appreciated each one. But a part of me kept waiting for that call from Anita that will never come again.

I think what I felt on that birthday must be just a small taste of what it feels like when you have lost a soul mate, to always be waiting for the call that never comes. You want that one special person to share every new experience, to have them by your side for the rest of your life. But the incontrovertible fact is that in one awful moment that became impossible. The call will not come. The presence you so desperately want is beyond your reach.

We cannot change the loss. That just is. But we each have a choice in how we continue to live without our loved one. On the one hand, we can permanently descend into the darkest depths of grief and stop allowing ourselves to experience anything new without them to share it with us. Or, we can venture out to embrace life as a tribute to the one who is gone, to see and do new things, and live for the both of you, if you will. And don't you think that whichever choice we make, existing in stasis or moving forward and living for two, our loved one's spirit is there beside us?

The choice is ours. I like to think they loved us enough to want us to live again. Anita was an adventurous woman, so I believe she would want to see what new experiences I can have for her.

Finding Your Way

Losing the love of your life can be one of the most solitary, lonely experiences you will ever know. While you may be surrounded by caring people who want to help you through your grief, at the end of the day, you are still alone. Your grief is unique to you. No one else will ever experience a sorrow quite like yours. You and the one you have lost were unique in the history of the world. How can anyone expect your grief to be anything but equally unique?

But still, you do not have to mourn alone. There are those out here who do understand. They have each experienced their own unique grief. And they can help you find your way in an unfamiliar solitary existence.

In many ways, grief can be like the changing faces of the ocean. In the early days, you may feel it is akin to a tidal wave sweeping in and engulfing you. You are tossed, helpless, in the waves, unable to breathe, to control your direction. Your only choice is to allow the turmoil to take you where it may. In its aftermath, thrown gasping on the shore of your life, you see only destruction and chaos wherever you look. But over time, you begin to rebuild, much like those communities that have lost all to the mighty wave. You will never be quite the same again, but in many ways, you will be stronger. And you will never forget.

Eventually, your life will begin to take on the ocean's gentler rhythms. You will be able to see a larger view to the blue horizon and perhaps understand a greater purpose for yourself as you come to terms with the new existence your loss has forced upon you. The ocean's beauty and majesty reassert themselves and your life goes on, one gentle swell after the other.

Oh, there will be times when the waves become stormy and your grief will threaten to overwhelm you once again, but storms do not last forever. The sun comes out, black clouds grow white, and blue skies do return. Treasure those days of sun. They are your respite from the sadness you have known. Allow yourself to wade in the gentle waves the ocean sends you that day. The soothing feel of the water on your feet, the sand beneath your toes, the breeze caressing your skin and ruffling your hair are all the stuff of healing.

Breathing Again

Climbing Off the Pity Pot

Like so many women, my friend, Anne, is a woman of many facets: wife, mother, teacher, artist, writer, accomplished musician, world traveler, and now a widow. Also like many women, when the widow mantle finally dropped over her head, most of her talents and interests had already been relegated to the background of her life. One at a time, her more creative sides took on a secondary role as she devoted herself to a husband who was slowly succumbing to Parkinson's disease. That disease and the decline that went hand in hand with it took center stage for over 16 years. And one sad day, she stepped from the role of devoted wife into the role of widow.

Now, through all that time, Anne never really let herself climb up onto a pity pot. She is usually a remarkably upbeat, positive woman. Surely the inclination for self-pity was there, and I'm pretty sure she did have her moments. Grief will do that. I suspect that in the quiet of her own home she wept and wished things could be different, but outside those walls, she kept up a brave front. I call that the *I'm fine* syndrome. Still, we knew she was desperately trying to find ways to mend her broken heart and learn to live as just Anne.

Cathy Marley

What she did do was force herself to take small steps out into the greater world around her. And like so many new widows, she moved from distraction to distraction, ever in search of something to fill the void. Early on, she took a trip abroad. It was one they had originally planned together but had delayed again and again in the face of illness. This time she went alone. It was something of a testament to the life they had dreamed of sharing in their later years, and I suppose, a small way to keep what she had lost alive.

She also redecorated her crafts room and began taking classes in new art forms she could embrace. Quilting took her attention for a while as did a book club. None really held her attention for long until one day she began talking again about her beloved violin.

That beautiful instrument was one of the first things she had put aside in the face of illness. Years had passed since this gifted musician, music teacher, and former concertmaster had touched its strings. The years in silence had affected her confidence, but those of us who cared deeply for her well-being in this new role as widow encouraged her to return to the healing powers of her music.

One evening she triumphantly announced that she had started to play again. With practice, her skills returned along with her confidence. A little at a time, we encouraged her to dare more public ways to play. And so, she did. She auditioned for a small community orchestra and was accepted—in the second violin section. It was a major step back for a woman who had once played first violin and conducted her own community's symphony orchestra.

From the perspective of grief, however, it was a major step forward to just move outside her sorrow, but it was still an ego blow that came when she was already fragile. That day, as she told me later, she realized she had taken the "demotion" harder than she thought she would. She went home and had a solo pity party, indulging in negative self-talk about not playing well anymore (not really true!), feeling she was a has-been (nope!), and feeling old and pushed aside (far from it!).

Perhaps most significantly of all, she realized she had once had an identity as a wife, but that identity was gone for good. Now she was a widow. I think that was ultimately the real cause of her unusual moment of self-pity. It was just easier to blame her changed circumstances as a musician than to face her sorrow and accept how deeply it was affecting her. After all, she thought she had been given more than enough time to prepare for it. But all the preparation in the world is not enough when it comes to the reality of death.

Once again, as she gave into that rare bout of self-pity, the specter of grief had raised its head and tried to drag her down to its depths. Intrepid woman that she is, she fought it and somehow managed to see beyond grief to the potential ahead. She realized finding happiness in the simple act of playing and immersing herself in her music was far more important than the status associated with one position or another.

Cathy Marley

I think grieving the death of a soul mate must leave you with that pity pot always lurking in the corners of your life. Just like a dark demon, it whispers invitations in your ear and suggests how easy it would be to just let go and, with no end in sight, feel sorry for yourself. Sometimes you will give in to the temptation. That is okay. It is normal to feel miserable when you have lost so much. The danger lies in settling in too comfortably on that pity pot and decorating the space around it with sadness draped in dark colors.

I believe Anne's example is a good one. She never let herself linger in that dark corner for too long. She allowed the self-pity and defeatism to have their rightful space but only for brief spells. In time, she planted a bright flower in the midst of her sorrow. That flower, for her, took the form of a beautiful violin and healing music flowing from its strings. Each of us has within ourselves our own equivalent of that violin. What is yours?

Smoothing the Sharp Edges of Grief

I have found that whenever I talk about the work we are doing with From Grief to Peace, what I say inevitably resonates at some level with the person I am talking to, as though I was guided to reach out at just that moment. Grief is universal. Everyone, it seems, is mourning someone they loved. Or they fear a loss that has yet to happen.

This past week, I was having my teeth cleaned and in casual, albeit garbled conversation, mentioned what we have been doing here and our purpose in doing it. Staci, the young hygienist asked me if a soul mate could only be a spouse. Then by way of example, she explained the deep emotional bond she has with her grandmother. It is, she believes, something that is far more profound than the usual grandmother-granddaughter connection.

My answer to Staci was that no, soul mates can be spouses, parents and children, siblings, even best friends. It is the soul connection that matters, not the one that is defined by social norms.

I immediately flashed on the recent loss of Carrie Fisher followed within a day by the death of her mother

Debbie Reynolds. There is no question in my mind that those two women were soul mates destined to be together in this lifetime. And when one was gone, the other simply could not go on without her. The jagged edges of her grief cut her deeply and that poor broken, bleeding heart carried them back to one another on a different plane.

That is one rare way to handle the loss of your soul mate.

Usually, the one left behind must find a way to carry on alone. The grief and finding your way to peace is a part of your soul's journey in this lifetime.

At first, you may feel as though the path beneath you is littered with broken glass, its sole purpose to make you bleed with every step you take. Just as the ocean's constant motion can soften the sharp edges on glass shards into smooth, lovely ocean glass, so too can surviving a profound loss (and the ups and downs that come with it) smooth your path from broken glass to softer sand. As you find a way to embrace your pain and let it be a part of who you are now, the pain will ease, the sharp edges will soften, and you will become stronger.

You are not the first to walk this painful path— nor will you be the last. When you are mourning the loss of your soul mate, it feels like you are the only one going on this incredibly painful journey. You feel alone, abandoned, adrift in life's ocean. Surely no one else could ever hurt as much or mourn as deeply. The loss of a soul mate generates such a heart-deep grief that it is hard to believe others could understand. You are not alone. There are others on the same path, and for some of them it has started to smooth. Look for them. They are reaching back to help you go forward.

Breathing Again

Old Spice for Steve

I remember Christmases with Steve. Steve was Norm's younger brother and mentally challenged. Although he was in his early thirties when I married Norm, I quickly realized that he would never be much older than sixteen. Forever a teenager, he could sometimes be socially inept. But he was always loving and especially giving. And so, Christmas with all its presents was his absolute favorite time of year.

Every Christmas, Steve would arrive at the family get together smelling strongly of his beloved Old Spice cologne and with carefully budgeted and selected gifts in hand. Usually, he could only afford to buy something—most often from his neighborhood Walgreen's—for the women in the family, but he never forgot us. And when he would arrive, he would be so excited about giving his gifts that he would insist we drop whatever we were doing and open his gift immediately. Yes, Steve loved Christmas. But he loved giving even more.

So, when Steve transitioned from us, is it any wonder that Christmas presents and the scent of Old Spice always made me think of Steve and his generous, loving heart? The first year after he died, I was determined to keep his spirit alive within the family.

Now, for many years, the adults in our family have agreed that none of us needs more stuff. Instead, we have opted for a silly gift exchange that involves drawing numbers and often stealing gifts that were opened before your number came up. And every year, Steve still gets to be a small part of the game. We put numbered slips of paper in a hat, and starting with the oldest person in the room, we each pick one. But I add a ringer. Among the numbers is one that says, "Steve."

Whoever draws Steve's name gets an extra gift that they are not to open. We all know what it is, after all. It is a wrapped bottle of Old Spice. With it comes the instruction that they are to pass the gift along to someone who would not otherwise receive a Christmas gift. It can be someone they know or a complete stranger. The important thing is that someone gets a surprise Christmas gift. And in that brief moment of passing forward an unexpected gift, Steve is a part of our Christmas once more.

Christmas is memories. It is tradition. And yet it is a time of year when the memories can be too painful to let us celebrate without a loved one who has transitioned. But it is also a time to remember sweet pasts when that person was with us. Those are the memories we treasure and maybe, just maybe, honoring the memories can ease the pain of loss just a little bit.

I don't know what memories you have of the people you loved who are no longer with you. I do know that they will always live in your heart. And perhaps you can still celebrate their most beautiful qualities by passing forward a little bit of the love they gave you when they were here. So, my question is, what is your Old Spice? What gift can you pass forward in honor of the one you have lost? Whatever it is, I believe your loved one's spirit will surely treasure that. And perhaps in giving that gift, your heart can find a small measure of peace in the memories it brings to mind.

Breathing Again

The Courage to Be Happy

One of America's favorite mothers died this week. The lovely and talented Florence Henderson, mother to *The Brady Bunch*, always seemed to be patient, kind, and tolerant with a lively, often fractious brood of kids. She was the mom many of us wished could be ours. After all, our own mothers were never that perfect. They had to write their own scripts, and frankly, some of them were not very good writers.

But I digress.

The fact is, we admired that perky, perpetually cheerful mother. But Carol Brady was the product of good writers. Florence Henderson, the woman, on the other hand, said something that affected me greatly. In yesterday's newspaper, they listed ten wise things she had said, some as Carol Brady, others from her own heart. Number 4 started me thinking about the path you must take to find peace after losing your soul mate.

After the death of her second husband, John Kappas, in 2012, she said, "It takes a lot of courage to be happy, but I've got courage, so I think I will be happy again."

Cathy Marley

I think I will be happy again. What a hopeful thing to say in a time of deep grieving. And what a gift to anyone going through the depths of loss.

It takes courage to simply put one foot in front of the other after you have lost your soul mate. But somehow you do it.

It takes courage to get up in the morning, day after day. But somehow you do it.

It takes courage to reclaim your life when all you want is to just stop and go to your love, wherever they are now. But somehow you find a way.

And it does take courage to find peace and happiness in the face of devastating loss. But you can do that, too.

At first, you cannot believe you will ever be happy again. But you will. It will sneak up on you. One day, you will read something funny or see something silly or flash to a happy memory, one not focused on death. And for just one brief moment, you will find yourself smiling or laughing. It will be the first time but not the last.

That laughter is not a betrayal of the one you love. Rather, it is an affirmation of the depth of the joy you experienced together. And having the courage to find your way to peace and be happy again is an even greater affirmation of the love you had and the life you shared. Cherish that and know that you DO have courage. You would not have survived through your loss without it.

Breathing Again

Photo by Kathy S.

Double the Joy

My friend Kathy's husband passed away over a year ago, and I find myself fascinated by how she has handled her loss. Her grief is something she keeps very much private and to all outward appearances, she is moving forward with life. I know she loved him deeply, and I know she misses him deeply, too. I am sure she has her times of tears. The fact that she is moving forward in no way dampens those feelings or the depth of her loss.

Cathy Marley

In many ways, she and her husband were very different individuals. They had a relationship based on mutual respect that gave them both the freedom to be who they were. They each celebrated life in ways that worked best for them individually and as a couple. A gregarious, social woman, Kathy has embraced life for as long as I have known her. She loves to travel and to get to know, really know, new people who become a part of her global social network. He, I think, preferred to be more of a homebody even though he happily traveled with her as often as he could. One thing is for sure. When they were together, they treasured every moment and created priceless memories.

So, I was not particularly surprised when Kathy told me about an exhilarating parasailing experience she had this summer in Central America. Her insights into the experience truly amazed me. As she flew high in the air, she said, she was incredibly thrilled by the adventure of what she was doing. In my mind, I can see her screaming in sheer joy, her face alight with excitement. But, in the midst of that joy, she sobered, feelings of guilt intruded, and tears came into her eyes as she realized she was doing it alone—that her husband was not there to share it with her. It dampened her enthusiasm and diminished the entire experience.

She later told a friend of her feelings. The feedback she got changed everything. Rather than feeling guilty for enjoying herself in her husband's absence, her friend suggested, perhaps it would be more valuable to understand she was doubling the joy by experiencing it for him as well.

Breathing Again

  I think perhaps for many people there is a feeling of guilt as they begin to live again. And living again is inevitable. But it can feel something like a betrayal of the person you loved so deeply. I would like to think that when you find yourself able to smile again, to laugh again, to find joy in even the smallest experience, you will cherish those things and know that in feeling joy once more, it is not a betrayal. Rather, you have doubled the joy as you embrace life in honor of the one you loved.

Breathing Again

Comfort Where You Find It

Some months ago, we adopted a sweet orphaned kitten. This tiny little boy had lost his mother—that first solid foundation—much too early in life. Whatever the circumstances that left him motherless also left him needy of the love and cuddling that helps all babies thrive. And so now, for whatever reason, Joe has adopted me as his surrogate mother. He snuggles and tries to nurse on any soft part of my body he can find. His favorite place is on my neck, close to the pulse just under my chin. There, he purrs and kneads and tries to suckle, butting his little head in search of a nipple he will never find. But the very act is a comfort to him.

Yesterday as I endured the discomfort of his sharp little claws and patiently waited for him to give up and settle for cuddling, I got to thinking about how very human he is in his need. I think we all rely on some solid foundation in life. It may start with our mother, but our ultimate solid ground is that soul mate we have come into this world seeking. Once we find him or her, we build a life on that foundation, one loving brick at a time, always trusting in its solidity. Our soul mate becomes more than a foundation. He or she becomes a touchstone we return to in any moment of need.

Cathy Marley

And so, it is no surprise that when you lose your soul mate, it feels like the very ground beneath your feet has started to shift, as though an earthquake has reached out and grabbed you, shaking and pulling in every direction at once. Suddenly, the world you trusted to always remain solid has become unreliable. From one heartbeat to the next, your foundation has been yanked away. The strong base on which you have built your world is gone, and you are left with nothing solid to cling to. Like our kitten, you are left adrift and unsure of what or who to trust.

None of us is ever ready for that to happen. Just as all the preparation in the world cannot diminish the shock of an earthquake, so, too, can the loss of your soul mate find you unprepared to lose the one person who would always be there for you in the roughest times. This is one of those times, and you need comfort to weather the storm but have no idea of where to find it.

I know a kitten losing its mother is no comparison to losing a soul mate. But his trusting nature and willingness to accept comfort where he finds it can serve as a valuable example. I may not be the ideal replacement for his feline mother, but I do represent a source of nurturing comfort. All creatures need that. So do you. As much as you have lost, you still need love. I am not saying you need to replace your soul mate. That is unlikely to happen, but opening your heart to the comfort offered by the friends and family who care for your well-being is a first step to finding the strength to move forward. It takes a little trust and as much vulnerability as you can manage. Just as our Joe finds comfort in faux-nursing a human mother who will never be the same as what he knew, so, too, can you find guilt-free comfort in the compassionate embrace of those who genuinely care and want nothing more than to help you find a new foundation for living again. Seeking comfort wherever you can find it is not a denial of what you had. Rather, accepting a comforting hand when it is offered and beginning to rebuild your life is an affirmation of the life you once knew.

Breathing Again

What Happened to Peace?

Lately, I have been thinking a lot about peace, on both a global and a personal level. I see people professing faith in God yet willing to hate or even kill their neighbors for differences over how to worship that God. And I want to weep for them. I see countries throwing peace away over power, greed or control, even leaders of countries willing to annihilate their own people for the same reasons. And I want to weep for them. And among individuals, I see spouses or siblings or families seeking revenge on one another for wrongs both large and small, imagined and real. And, yes, I want to weep for them as well. What happened to their peace?

It seems as though they are not willing to let go of their hurt, or their hatred, or their position for even the moment it takes to try understanding a different point of view. And they all miss out on peace in one way or another.

But peace is more than just the absence of war or strife. It is peace of mind as well, a hard-earned inner calmness and acceptance of what is.

I do know one thing for sure. On an individual

level, we sometimes become complacent when things are going well. Our lives are working, and we feel some measure of happiness. I don't know about you, but being loved and feeling loved in return goes a long way toward that happiness for me. Take the love away, and peace disappears as though a magician has stepped in with some cosmic sleight of hand trick. Your world is rocked to its very foundations, and in the face of overwhelming grief, peace seems impossible. The road back to it quickly becomes rocky and difficult. I have seen my friends struggle to move forward along that path, and I have developed a great empathy for what they have endured as they seek some new measure of peace.

I still believe with all my heart that peace is possible. The challenge on a global level is undeniably complex and difficult. That is beyond my abilities. But one person at a time, I can step onto that rocky path and walk beside those I love, those who have lost sight of peace as they grieve. They do not have to make the journey alone.

Perhaps that is one way we can encourage peace around the world. It starts with one heart at a time. On a personal level, it starts with those who are grieving and those who have yet to grieve. We can reach out and hold our neighbor's hands in understanding and love. Start with those closest to us and reach out until we have reached around the world.

Choosing Love

Over the last couple of weeks, I have become aware that I am grumpier and more negative than I think I have ever been before. I think I have been absorbing far too much of the anger that seems to permeate the world around me. I watch the news, read the newspaper, and follow posts on Facebook daily. And frankly, what I see is not happy. I'm not even sure why I keep doing this. It is somewhat like having a sore tooth that I keep poking at to see if it still hurts. It does. Always.

If the world around me wants to go that way, so be it. However, I am making a choice to check out of the anger, the negativity, the pessimism, as much as I can. Why? Because I want to make the best of the time I have with those I love. I do not know how much time I have left with them. I do not know if I will transition first or they will. So why should I waste the precious time we have together reflecting a world angst that makes me unhappy with everything and everyone?

I find myself thinking of those who have left us. I am confident that all of them left when the world was in the midst of one crisis, one controversy or another. That is the way the world works and it always will. Crisis and dissention are a part of life. I also believe that all of those who have passed left behind someone who grieves deeply and wishes he or she just had one more hour, one more day together to spend in some lighthearted connection, some time when the most important thing was how much they cared for one another.

Those who are gone are no longer wrapped up in the petty differences that tend to consume so many of us in this life. Who is or is not President is not their concern. Who fails to follow through on their promises is not their concern either. Nor are they really worried about who lives where or believes what. They have a much deeper understanding of this life than we do. Their perspective is, I believe, more global. They see the larger picture.

I know our loved ones are now in a place where one emotion and one emotion only rules. Love. If love is the end result for us all, then why not start now?

Photo by Cathy Marley

Epilogue for Dale

When I first started writing the stories for this book, what I knew about grief was learned mostly secondhand from the experiences of my two friends who had both lost soul mates. They were grieving deeply, and I wanted nothing more than to find a way to help them through that dark landscape to some measure of peace. Little did I know that in helping them I was building strength to eventually help me in my own dark days of sorrow—days I did not see coming at the time.

I believe God, or the Universe, or the spirit world, whatever you choose to believe, sends us ways to be strong in the most difficult times. Our guides see what we are going through in our grief and enfold us in their protective embrace. We may not always see it, but it is there. We have but to pay attention and reach out when that aid is offered. In it lies solace.

As a child, I knew sorrow when my mother died, but I had long buried that grief, putting it behind me as though it belonged with my childhood. I knew that eventually, as an adult, I would someday mourn again. Like most of us, I went through my days blissfully and vainly hoping I could keep avoiding that ultimately unavoidable fact of life. And sure enough, my time came, too.

I am thankful that my exposure to sorrow has come late in what has generally been a happy, blessed life, and that it came gradually. I am also thankful for my guardian spirits in the afterlife who sent me signs of their presence and loving support both before and after losses that seemed to escalate in intensity. At first, I am sure I did not notice the signs, but in time I did. Recognizing them and knowing what I had learned about the afterlife gave me the comfort I needed when sorrow struck. The work I had been doing with both Joy and Betts had taught me the effects grief can have on our existence and prepared me for them when they came into my own life. Oh yes, I recognized grief when it came knocking at my door.

Looking back, I can see that each dose of sorrow was more painful than the one before. Each one prepared me for the greater loss to come. I do not mean to diminish any one of the losses I experienced as I was writing this book. Each one hurt in its own way. It's just that each loss seemed to hurt more deeply than the last. Perhaps grief is cumulative. I really hope not. But if it is, there is some small consolation in having built strong scar tissue around my heart before the most profound loss yet, my son, Dale.

Each time sorrow came calling, it was because I had lost someone very important to me. It started, as you have read here, with one very special pet, my Beau. I hoped that was the worst grief I would ever have to know before I reached the end of my own life, but in my heart, I knew it was not.

And then Anita died. Knowing I would never see her again, never again hear her musical laughter, never again feel her warm, all-encompassing hugs, I felt a huge Anita-shaped void in my heart and was sure the pain had taken up permanent residence there. Yet a spirit dream visit eased the sorrow by letting me know how content she is now in the afterlife. You have read about that here, too. So yes, I was better prepared than most, but as anyone who has lost a loved one will tell you, you are never prepared for that person to leave.

And then there was Dale, our funny, sweet, generous son. His was the most sorrowful, most profound loss yet. As I write this, my heart is still raw, and tears come when I least expect them. Anything can set me off—a silly toy, an Air Force Veteran ball cap, a photograph of happy times, remembering his goofy smile, even a can of generic cheap beer. Anything. I know I am still grieving his absence. I think I always will.

The last five months of Dale's life were like living on a perpetual rollercoaster. When he was first diagnosed with cancer, we happily announced to the world that his prognosis for recovery was excellent. After all, that is what the doctors said, and we desperately wanted to believe them. He had surgery to remove one tumor, started radiation for another, and quickly began showing signs of recovery. But then the headaches returned, and he was back in the hospital. Then he was out and then back in again. With each hospital stay, there seemed to be just a little less of the Dale we knew. The ups and downs came with increasingly shorter time in between, until finally one sad morning, we heard *hospice* and before we knew it, he was gone. I wish I could have done more to ease his last days.

Publishing *Breathing Again* is proving to be a bittersweet effort. When I published my first book, *Peeking Over the Edge*, Dale proudly announced my accomplishment to everyone he met. It was as though he thought I had hung the moon. Maybe in his eyes, I had. So, when I told him about this newest book, he again bragged about it to everyone he knew. After he died, I knew that somehow, I had to set my grief aside and find the strength and the courage to keep writing and complete all the final steps I needed to take to bring this book to print. I think I owed it to Dale. As I have slowly made my way to finishing, I have felt him beside me with each step, cheering every word I wrote.

I am not sure I would have made it to print through my grief without the sense of what it meant to Dale. And I know his spiritual encouragement was there. In a recent group reading with Susanne Wilson, the Carefree Medium, I got a message from a spirit I am convinced was Dale. There was little time in the group setting but by sending Susanne an image of him looking over the edge of a cliff (my first book, remember, was titled *Peeking Over the Edge*), he did manage to make the connection to my writing and my books. I feel strongly that he wanted me to know how important it is for me to finish this book and put it into the hands of those who are grieving and those who want to support someone they love who is grieving.

So, for you Dale, here it finally is!

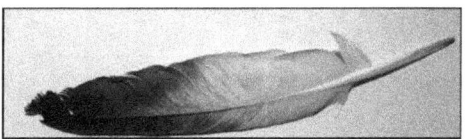

Photo by Cathy Marley

A gift from Dale on the day Breathing Again was complete.

Photo by Rita Sherman, Captured Moments

About the Author

Cathy Marley is an award-winning freelance writer/author, entrepreneur, wife, mother, grandmother, and great-grandmother. She lives a contented life in Phoenix, Arizona, with Norm, her soul mate and husband of over forty-four years. Fur babies Jake and Molly the dogs, Sugar the cat, and Joe the cat who thinks he is a dog, make for an exciting household. Cathy and Norm's extended family includes Norm's three (now only two on this side) adult children, seven adult grandchildren, and at last count, 14 great grandchildren.

Cathy Marley

A former aerospace techie, Cathy dismissed her creative talents for most of her professional life until she discovered a passion for writing in midlife. She was first published in ***Love in Bloom***, a creative collection of essays, short stories, and poetry from Women Writers of the Desert. Shortly thereafter, Cathy wrote and published ***Peeking Over the Edge...views from life's middle***, a collection of her own reflections on life as she reached middle-age.

As a member of Women Writers of the Desert, Cathy formed a friendship with fellow writers Joy Collins and Betts McCalla. That friendship deepened after both Betts and Joy suffered the loss of their husbands and soul mates. As their friend, Cathy sought ways to help them work through their grief and find peace. From Grief to Peace, the company they founded to help others who are grieving, and this book arose from that time. ***Breathing Again – thoughts on life after loss*** was written from the perspective of someone who wants to understand what a grieving friend is experiencing, and in the truest spirit of friendship, provide love and support as that friend finds his or her way to peace.

You can contact Cathy Marley at:
CJM@CathyMarley.com
or through her website:
www.CathyMarley.com

www.ingramcontent.com/pod-product-compliance
Lightning Source LLC
Chambersburg PA
CBHW070607300426
44113CB00010B/1436